53
Interesting Ways
to Appraise
Your Teaching

53
Interesting Ways
to Appraise
Your Teaching

Graham Gibbs
Professor & Director,
Centre for Higher Education Practice,
Open University

Sue Habeshaw
Senior Lecturer, Faculty of Humanities,
University of the West of England, Bristol

Trevor Habeshaw
TES Ltd. &
University of Exeter

Technical and Educational Services Ltd.
First published in 1987 by
Technical and Educational Services Ltd.
37 Ravenswood Road
Bristol BS6 6BW
UK

© 1988 Graham Gibbs, Sue Habeshaw, Trevor Habeshaw

Reprinted 1989, 1997

ISBN 0 947885 27 7

Printed in Great Britain by The Cromwell Press, Melksham, Wiltshire

TES Books are distributed by
Plymbridge Distributors Ltd.
Estover
Plymouth PL6 7PZ

For Customer Services
telephone +44 (0) 1752 202301 or fax orders +44 (0) 1752 202333

Books from Technical & Educational Services

The 53 series
53 Interesting Things to Do in Your Lectures
53 Interesting Things to Do in Your Seminars and Tutorials
53 Interesting Ways to Assess Your Students
53 Interesting Ways of Helping Your Students to Study
53 Interesting Communication Exercises for Science Students
53 Interesting Ways to Teach Mathematics
53 Problems with Large Classes: *Making the Best of a Bad Job*
53 Interesting Ways to Write Open Learning Materials
53 Interesting Activities for Open Learning Courses
53 Interesting Ways to Promote Equal Opportunities in Education
53 Questions and Answers about Semesters and Modules
53 Interesting Ways to Supervise Student Projects, Dissertations and Theses

Interesting ways to teach
Preparing to Teach: An Introduction to Effective Teaching in Higher Education
253 Ideas for Your Teaching
Interesting Ways to Teach: 12 Do-It-Yourself Staff Development Exercises

Other titles
Getting the Most from Your Data: Practical Ideas on how to Analyse Qualitative Data
Writing Study Guides
Improving the Quality of Student Learning
Teaching University Students Chemistry
Essential Chemistry for Advanced Biologists
HMA Stationery Ltd.

Contents   Page

Appraisal interviews

About the series

These books are intended for teachers in further and higher education, though they are equally suitable for nurse tutors, management trainers and instructors on government training projects. Teachers in schools, too, will be able to adapt the material to their own situations.

The purpose of the series is to provide teachers with practical ideas for their teaching. While there are sound theoretical justifications for the suggestions (and occasionally even empirical evidence in their support) the emphasis throughout is on practice. The methods have all been tried out, and seen to work, by the authors.

The authors run workshops in the methods described in the books and full instructions for do-it-yourself training workshops are obtainable from the publishers. (The address is on page 4.)

Acknowledgements

We have not invented all the ideas in this book ourselves. We are grateful to colleagues and friends who told us about methods which they had encountered or invented. We are glad to acknowledge these but are aware that some remain unacknowledged. If readers who recognise any of the unattributed ideas will send us a note of the source, we will happily add an acknowledgement in the next edition of the book.

Graham Gibbs, Sue Habeshaw & Trevor Habeshaw
July 1988

Introduction

This book was written in 1989 in response to the growing interest in the appraisal of teaching, both on the part of teachers themselves and their managers. In higher education this was encouraged first by CNAA and other validating bodies, especially following the introduction of Partnership in Validation and 'progress review', and was later extensively used in work in the mid to late 1990's which preceded the departmental self-assessments conducted under the aegis of the Higher Education Funding Councils in England, Wales and Scotland

Teachers were looking for interesting and effective methods to use in the appraisal of their teaching and our initial response was to put together this collection of 53 practical suggestions. Each was written to make sense on its own, though they are arranged in chapters and cross-refer where appropriate.

This reprint, as before, is addressed to the individual teacher though it includes suggestions of how teams can work together to appraise their courses. The ideas can also be adapted for use in staff development workshops. Heads of department and others with an appraising role will be able to use the book to help their staff.

Several thousand copies of this book have been sold since 1989 and much has been learned since this time which will be incorporated into the fully revised second edition planned for 1999. Meanwhile, for those teachers who wish right now to appraise their work more systematically, the items in this volume remain a very useful starting point.

Trevor Habeshaw July 1997

Appraisal using questionnaires

A simple questionnaire

The questionnaire which follows was developed at the Curtin University of Technology, Australia[1]. It forms part of a range of devices offered by a centralised evaluation service and has been used in promotion procedures. It is meant to be used for a quick check on overall teacher performance and is a good example of a well designed questionnaire.

If you want to use this questionnaire, or design your own to this model, you may find the following points helpful.

a In this questionnaire each item is expressed in two different ways. This helps students to see exactly what is being asked.

b It is very difficult for any brief set of teacher rating scales not to embody particular values or assumptions about how teaching ought to be conducted. The set here is better than most in this respect but still appears to assume that the teacher is solely responsible for course organisation, presentation of material and feedback to students. If you are facilitating a student-centred course you will need to add your own items to the questionnaire.

c Student ratings of teachers are influenced by context. For example a compulsory first year course with a large enrolment may get poorer ratings than an optional third year course with a small student group taught by the same teacher. Similarly an average teacher in a department where teaching is generally poor may receive better ratings than a good teacher in a department where teaching is generally excellent. This means that any particular teacher's ratings from a particular course should be interpreted with great care. Ideally you would compare them with ratings of other teachers who have taught similar courses and ratings of the same teacher

---

1 Reproduced with the permission of the Educational Development Unit, Curtin University of Technology, Perth

on different courses. The wording of item 6 on the questionnaire attempts to take these problems into account by asking students to make a comparative rating 'taking into account the nature and relative difficulty of this unit'.

d   Before administering a questionnaire, you should clarify who will own the results, and who else will have legitimate access to them. Otherwise they may be used in insensitive and unintelligent ways, by people other than those for whom they were obtained. You might decide, for example, that it will be acceptable for individuals to access their own ratings and the average ratings of their colleagues, but unacceptable for anyone to have access to other individuals' ratings.

Questionnaire: student appraisal of lecturers

1 **Organisation**
   The lecturer gives direction as necessary, ensuring that the requirements of the unit are clear.
   With this lecturer I know what I'm supposed to be doing.

2 **Feedback**
   The lecturer provides meaningful, adequate and prompt feedback.
   This lecturer keeps me in the picture about how I'm doing.

3 **Knowledge of subject**
   The lecturer has command of the subject material.
   This lecturer obviously knows what s/he's talking about.

4 **Communication**
   The lecturer effectively communicates what s/he's trying to teach.
   This lecturer really gets the message across.

5 **Responsiveness**
   The lecturer is responsive to student needs at an individual and group level.
   This lecturer shows a genuine concern for students.

6 **This lecturer compared with others**
   In the light of the previous items, and taking into account the nature and relative difficulty of this unit, how do you rate this lecturer compared with other lecturers you have had?

Lecturer ....

Make your response like this: 1   2   3   ④   5

	Aspect	**High**				**Low**
1	Organisation	1	2	3	4	5
2	Feedback	1	2	3	4	5
3	Knowledge of subject	1	2	3	4	5
4	Communication	1	2	3	4	5
5	Responsiveness	1	2	3	4	5
6	This lecturer cf. others	1	2	3	4	5

Diagnostic questionnaire 2

A drawback of standard lecture feedback questionnaires is that, because for practical reasons the number of questions has to be limited, the focus of the questions is inevitably broad. This means that, though responses to such questionnaires may indicate where problems lie, they take the teacher no further forward in understanding the cause of a problem or knowing what to do about it. For this, more detailed feedback is called for. One way of obtaining this is through a method known as 'progressive focussing' **(see 43)**.

The questionnaire which follows[1] looks like a standard general purpose lecture feedback questionnaire. In fact it has a diagnostic function and is the first of a set of nine questionnaires, the other eight of which are used to follow up the issues which are identified. For example you might obtain the following response to item 11 in the diagnostic questionnaire from your 58 students:

The lecturer:	strongly agree	agree	neither agree nor disagree	disagree	strongly disagree
11 has a wide knowledge of his/her subject	1	4	7	27	19

This would indicate a need to find out why you give this impression. One of the eight follow-up questionnaires is concerned specifically with student perceptions of the lecturer's knowledge of the subject, and contains 13 items, such as:

The lecturer:
relies on textbooks for lecturing
can answer questions off the cuff

---

1   Reproduced with the permission of the Department of Educational Studies, University of Surrey

Students' responses to these more detailed items would provide you with a fuller picture of what is going on and help you find a solution to the problem.

The way the follow-up questionnaires relate to items in the diagnostic questionnaire can be seen in the following table.

Follow-up questionnaire		Item(s) on the diagnostic questionnaire
2	Lecturer's knowledge of the subject	11
3	Maintenance of student interest during lectures	12, 13
4	Note taking in lectures	8, 9, 10
5	Clarity and comprehensibility of lecture	14, 15, 16, 17
6	Lecturer's enthusiasm for the subject	18
7	Students' perception of the lecturer	3, 4
8	Lecturer's attitude to students	5, 6, 7
9	Encouragement of student participation in lectures	1, 2

These questionnaires are available from:
The Administrator, CATHE
Department of Educational Studies (AA)
University of Surrey
Guildford, Surrey, GU2 5XH

Reference
D McConnell and V Hodgson,   'The development of student constructed feedback questionnaires', *Assessment and Evaluation in Higher Education*, 10, 2-27

Diagnostic lecture questionnaire

The lecturer:	strongly agree	agree	neither agree nor disagree	disagree	strongly disagree
1 encourages student participation in lectures	....	....	....	....	....
2 allows opportunities for asking questions	....	....	....	....	....
3 has a good lecture delivery	....	....	....	....	....
4 has a good rapport with students	....	....	....	....	....
5 is approachable and friendly with students	....	....	....	....	....
6 is respectful towards students	....	....	....	....	....
7 is able to reach the students' level	....	....	....	....	....
8 enables easy note-taking	....	....	....	....	....
9 provides useful printed notes*	....	....	....	....	....
10 could help students by providing printed notes	....	....	....	....	....
11 has a wide knowledge of his/her subject	....	....	....	....	....
12 maintains student interest during lectures	....	....	....	....	....
13 gives varied, lively lectures	....	....	....	....	....
14 is clear and comprehensible in lectures	....	....	....	....	....
15 gives lectures which are too fast to take in	....	....	....	....	....
16 gives audible lectures	....	....	....	....	....
17 gives structured, organised lectures	....	....	....	....	....
18 appears to be enthusiastic for the subject	....	....	....	....	....

* Please answer if applicable

Study questionnaire 3

Students study in different ways and with varying degrees of success. Since the way they approach their studying is directly affected by the way in which they are taught, a questionnaire which evaluates study methods not only provides useful feedback to students but also offers a valuable opportunity for the appraisal of teaching.

A questionnaire entitled *Approaches to Studying* [1], which is based on extensive research on differences in the ways students study, has been developed at the University of Lancaster. It has been used extensively in a large number of university and polytechnic departments and there are national norms available for different subject areas. A short version of the questionnaire follows, together with full instructions for scoring and interpreting the results. This version contains 18 questions and produces scores on three scales.

Scale A   **Achieving orientation**
This measures the extent to which students are competitive, well organised and concerned to do well.

Scale B   **Reproducing orientation**
This measures the extent to which students are attempting to memorise the subject matter

Scale C   **Meaning orientation**
This measures the extent to which students are attempting to make sense of the subject matter.

1   Reproduced with the permission of Noel Entwistle and Paul Ramsden

It has been found that students who have a high score on the 'reproducing orientation' scale get poorer results, have higher failure rates and tend not to understand ideas or be able to relate them or draw conclusions from them.

The questionnaire has been used as a course evaluation device to measure the effects of different kinds of teaching on student learning. For example, in one polytechnic evaluation where students in 24 different subject areas completed the questionnaire, it was found that their approach to study was clearly related to how much time they spent in class: students on courses with relatively low class contact hours tended to have higher scores on 'meaning orientation', and those on courses with high contact hours had higher scores on 'reproducing orientation'.

This questionnaire is more appropriately used for diagnostic self-appraisal purposes than for comparisons. You can use it, for example, to measure the effect on your students' approach to study of any changes which you introduce into your teaching.

The relationship between student learning and characteristics of courses can be investigated using a second questionnaire, the *Course perceptions questionnaire* **(see 4)**.

The research and theoretical background to the questionnaires can be found in:

N J Entwistle and P Ramsden, *Understanding Student Learning*,
Croom Helm, London, 1983

Questionnaire: Approaches to studying

Please answer every item quickly by giving your immediate response. Circle the appropriate code number to show your general approach to studying.

4 (++) means *definitely agree*

3 (+) means *agree with reservations*

2 (?) is only to be used if the item doesn't apply to you or if you find it impossible to give a definite answer.

1 (-) means *disagree with reservations*

0 (- -) means *definitely disagree*

		++	+	?	-	--	
1	I find it easy to organise my study time effectively.	4	3	2	1	0	(A)
2	I like to be told precisely what to do in essays or other set work.	4	3	2	1	0	(B)
3	It's important to me to do really well in the courses here.	4	3	2	1	0	(A)
4	I usually set out to understand thoroughly the meaning of what I am asked to read.	4	3	2	1	0	(C)
5	When I'm reading I try to memorise important facts which may come in useful later.	4	3	2	1	0	(B)
6	When I'm doing a piece of work, I try to bear in mind exactly what that particular lecturer seems to want.	4	3	2	1	0	(A)
7	My main reason for being here is so that I can learn more about the subjects which really interest me.	4	3	2	1	0	(C)
8	I suppose I'm more interested in the qualifications I'll get than in the courses I'm taking.	4	3	2	1	0	(B)
9	I'm usually prompt in starting work in the evenings.	4	3	2	1	0	(A)
10	I generally put a lot of effort into trying to understand things which initially seem difficult.	4	3	2	1	0	(C)
11	Often I find I have to read things without having a chance to really understand them.	4	3	2	1	0	(B)
12	If conditions aren't right for me to study, I generally manage to do something to change them.	4	3	2	1	0	(A)
13	I often find myself questioning things that I hear in lessons/lectures or read in books.	4	3	2	1	0	(C)

		++	+	?	-	--	
14	I tend to read very little beyond what's required for completing assignments.	4	3	2	1	0	(B)
15	It is important to me to do things better than my friends, if I possibly can.	4	3	2	1	0	(A)
16	I spend a good deal of my spare time in finding out more about interesting topics which have been discussed in class.	4	3	2	1	0	(C)
17	I find academic topics so interesting, I should like to continue with them after I finish this course.	4	3	2	1	0	(C)
18	I find I have to concentrate on memorising a good deal of what we have to learn.	4	3	2	1	0	(B)

Score sheet

Score your questionnaire by writing down the numbers circled for questions marked A, B or C. There should be six numbers for each. Then add up the totals for the columns A, B and C.

A	B	C
TOTALS		

'A' scale score

This is a score out of 24 on 'achieving orientation'. This indicates competitiveness, well organised study methods, and hope for success. Students who score high on this scale are oriented towards doing well, whatever this involves. They tend to do well. (Correlation between scale score and success rating = +0.32)

'B' scale score

This is a score out of 24 on 'reproducing orientation'. This indicates a surface approach to learning. Students who score high on this scale attempt to memorise subject matter and are not interested in studying a subject for its own sake but only out of a concern to pass or gain qualifications. They keep narrowly to the syllabus as laid down in course descriptions and do not follow up interests of their own (if they have any). Despite their concern to pass they tend to do badly. (Correlation between scale score and success rating = -0.25)

'C' scale score

This is a score out of 24 on 'meaning orientation'. This indicates a deep approach to learning: the intention to make sense of the subject, an interest in the subject itself, and a desire to learn. Students who score high on this scale follow up their own interests even if these are outside those parts of the course which are assessed. They tend to do well. (Correlation between scale score and success rating = +0.28)

Norms are available from large-scale national studies of how students learn, so you can compare your scores with national averages:

	Scale	Arts	Social science	Science	Overall	Standard deviation
A	Achieving	12.50	12.73	13.08	12.82	4.26
B	Reproducing	11.98	13.65	14.26	13.51	4.40
C	Meaning	15.17	14.21	13.93	14.31	4.51
Predictor of success		15.69	13.29	12.75	13.62	

Course perceptions questionnaire 4

The *Course perceptions questionnaire*[1], like the *Approaches to studying* questionnaire (**see 3**) was developed at Lancaster University and is based on research into students' perceptions of the context in which they study. It is more appropriately used for diagnostic purposes than for comparisons between courses. A copy of the questionnaire follows.

The questionnaire has 40 items and produces scores on 8 sub-scales. These are labelled A - H and are indicated in the right-hand column of the questionnaire.

A   Formal teaching methods

B   Clear goals and standards

C   Workload

D   Good teaching

E   Freedom in learning

F   Openness to students

G   Social climate

H   Vocational relevance

This questionnaire has been used in a large number of university and polytechnic departments and there are national norms available for each of the sub-scales for a range of subject areas.

A description of the use of this questionnaire can be found in:

P Ramsden and   'Effects of academic departments on students' approaches to studying'
N J Entwistle,   *British Journal of Educational Psychology*, 51, 368-383, 1981

1   Reproduced with the permission of Noel Entwistle and Paul Ramsden

Course perceptions questionnaire

4 (++) means *definitely agree*

3 (+)   means *agree with reservations*

2 (?)   is only to be used if the item doesn't apply to you or if you find it impossible to give a definite answer

1 (-)   means *disagree with reservations*

0 (- -) means *definitely disagree*

		++	+	?	-	- -	
1	A great deal of my time is taken up by timetabled classes (lectures, practicals, tutorials etc).	4	3	2	1	0	(A)
2	There is a real opportunity on this course for students to choose the particular areas they want to study.	4	3	2	1	0	(E)
3	Lecturers here frequently give the impression that they haven't anything to learn from students.	4	3	2	1	0	(D*)
4	You usually have a clear idea of where you're going and what's expected of you on this course.	4	3	2	1	0	(B)
5	A lot of students on this course are friends of mine.	4	3	2	1	0	(G)
6	The workload here is too heavy.	4	3	2	1	0	(C)
7	Most of the staff here are receptive to suggestions from students for changes in their teaching methods.	4	3	2	1	0	(F)
8	The course is geared to students' future employment.	4	3	2	1	0	(H)
9	You can learn nearly everything you need to know from the classes and lectures; it isn't necessary to do much further reading.	4	3	2	1	0	(A)

		++	+	-	- -	?	
10	The course really seems to encourage us to develop our own academic interests as far as possible.	4	3	2	1	0	(E)
11	Most of the staff here seem to prepare their teaching very thoroughly.	4	3	2	1	0	(D)
12	It's always easy here to know the standard of work expected of you.	4	3	2	1	0	(B)
13	Students from this course often get together socially.	4	3	2	1	0	(G)
14	It sometimes seems to me that the syllabus tries to cover too many topics.	4	3	2	1	0	(C)
15	Staff here generally consult students before making decisions about how the course is organised.	4	3	2	1	0	(F)
16	Lecturers on this course are keen to point out that they are giving us a professional training.	4	3	2	1	0	(H)
17	On this course you are expected to spend a lot of time studying on your own.	4	3	2	1	0	(A*)
18	We seem to be given a lot of choice here in the work we have to do.	4	3	2	1	0	(E)
19	Lecturers on this course seem to be good at pitching their teaching at the right level for us.	4	3	2	1	0	(D)
20	It's hard to tell how well you are doing on this course.	4	3	2	1	0	(B*)
21	This course seems to foster a friendly climate which helps students to get to know each other.	4	3	2	1	0	(G)
22	There is so much written work to be done that it is very difficult to get down to independent reading.	4	3	2	1	0	(C)

		++	+	-	- -	?	
23	Most of the lecturers here try really hard to get to know students.	4	3	2	1	0	(F)
24	The course seems to be pretty well determined by vocational requirements.	4	3	2	1	0	(H)
25	The lectures on this course are basically a guide to reading.	4	3	2	1	0	(A*)
26	This course gives you a chance to use methods of study which suit your own way of learning.	4	3	2	1	0	(E)
27	Staff here make a real effort to understand difficulties students may be having.	4	3	2	1	0	(D)
28	Lecturers here usually tell students exactly what they are supposed to be learning.	4	3	2	1	0	(B)
29	This course organises meetings and talks which are usually well attended.	4	3	2	1	0	(G)
30	There seems to be too much work to get through on the course.	4	3	2	1	0	(C)
31	Lecturers on this course seem to go out of their way to be friendly towards students.	4	3	2	1	0	(F)
32	The work I do here will definitely improve my future employment prospects.	· 4	3	2	1	0	(H)
33	Lectures seem to be more important than tutorials or discussion groups on this course.	4	3	2	1	0	(A)
34	Students have a great deal of choice over how they are going to learn on this course.	4	3	2	1	0	(E)
35	The lecturers on this course always seem ready to give help and advice on approaches to studying.	4	3	2	1	0	(D)
36	There's a lot of pressure on you as a student here.	4	3	2	1	0	(C)

		++	+	-	--	?	
37	Students on this course frequently discuss their work with each other.	4	3	2	1	0	(G)
38	Lecturers here generally make it clear right from the start what will be required of students.	4	3	2	1	0	(B)
39	There seems to be considerable emphasis here on inculcating the 'right' professional attitudes.	4	3	2	1	0	(H)
40	Lecturers on this course generally take students' ideas and interests seriously.	4	3	2	1	0	(F)

* The scale scores are reversed for asterisked items: 0 1 2 3 4

Computer-aided questionnaires 5

There are several ways in which computers are commonly used to assist student appraisal of teachers.

a Cafeteria questionnaires

In the cafeteria system, a large bank of tried and tested questionnaire items is held in a data base. These items are commonly grouped in sections according to topic, e.g. seminars, lectures etc. Teachers access the data base and select a sub-set of items to suit their specific purposes. This sub-set is then automatically printed out in an appropriate layout with spaces for students' responses.

The cafeteria system saves teachers the trouble of inventing questionnaire items and designing and typing their own questionnaires. It has the added advantage that items have already been tested and 'de-bugged'.

b Terminal-based data collection

In some systems, once the selection of items has been made, the questionnaire is available to students on terminals. Students can log in, access the questionnaire and key in their responses, even typing in open-ended responses. The data can be stored in a file for subsequent analysis and access can be restricted by use of a password. This system means that no printing of questionnaires is necessary and the collation and analysis of data can be automatic.

c Optical mark reading

More commonly, students are presented with printed questionnaires and fill in their responses on a special sheet which can be read automatically by an optical mark reader. An example of a typical optical mark reader form follows. Students may be instructed to complete only selected sections of the form, for example only those sections on tutorials and seminars. The pile of completed forms is stacked in the optical mark reader and read automatically. Most commercial models include a standard analysis programme and produce a full print-out of the results. This is probably the most flexible and most useful computer application to implement, though the initial cost of hardware may be high.

d   Statistical packages

Teachers who do not have access to an optical mark reader may need to number their questionnaire items for coding. Once in a data file the responses can be analysed using a standard statistical package. Teachers who are lucky enough to have a data preparation service in their institution can ask the staff to advise on the choice of coding instructions. Otherwise they can use a simple statistical package on a microcomputer (e.g. STATWORKS on an Apple Macintosh) and enter the data themselves.

e   Integrated systems

Full-blown computer-based systems integrate questionnaire design, printing, data entry, storage and analysis. They allow statistical comparisons to be made between teachers and between courses, as well as longer-term comparisons of the operation of a course in different years. A problem with integrated systems is that if they are sufficiently flexible to allow users to explore what they are interested in, then they are likely to be complicated. Such systems also have the drawback that they make it very easy to collect large amounts of data which are of little use but which accrue a spurious credibility simply because of the technology involved.

CANDIDATE SURNAME | INITS.

SUBJECT

cAɔ cAɔ cAɔ cAɔ cAɔ cAɔ cAɔ cAɔ cAɔ cAɔ cAɔ cAɔ cAɔ cAɔ cAɔ cAɔ cAɔ cAɔ cAɔ cAɔ
cBɔ cBɔ cBɔ cBɔ cBɔ cBɔ cBɔ cBɔ cBɔ cBɔ cBɔ cBɔ cBɔ cBɔ cBɔ cBɔ cBɔ cBɔ cBɔ cBɔ
cCɔ cCɔ cCɔ cCɔ cCɔ cCɔ cCɔ cCɔ cCɔ cCɔ cCɔ cCɔ cCɔ cCɔ cCɔ cCɔ cCɔ cCɔ cCɔ cCɔ
cDɔ cDɔ cDɔ cDɔ cDɔ cDɔ cDɔ cDɔ cDɔ cDɔ cDɔ cDɔ cDɔ cDɔ cDɔ cDɔ cDɔ cDɔ cDɔ cDɔ
cEɔ cEɔ cEɔ cEɔ cEɔ cEɔ cEɔ cEɔ cEɔ cEɔ cEɔ cEɔ cEɔ cEɔ cEɔ cEɔ cEɔ cEɔ cEɔ cEɔ
cFɔ cFɔ cFɔ cFɔ cFɔ cFɔ cFɔ cFɔ cFɔ cFɔ cFɔ cFɔ cFɔ cFɔ cFɔ cFɔ cFɔ cFɔ cFɔ cFɔ
cGɔ cGɔ cGɔ cGɔ cGɔ cGɔ cGɔ cGɔ cGɔ cGɔ cGɔ cGɔ cGɔ cGɔ cGɔ cGɔ cGɔ cGɔ cGɔ cGɔ
cHɔ cHɔ cHɔ cHɔ cHɔ cHɔ cHɔ cHɔ cHɔ cHɔ cHɔ cHɔ cHɔ cHɔ cHɔ cHɔ cHɔ cHɔ cHɔ cHɔ
cIɔ cIɔ cIɔ cIɔ cIɔ cIɔ cIɔ cIɔ cIɔ cIɔ cIɔ cIɔ cIɔ cIɔ cIɔ cIɔ cIɔ cIɔ cIɔ cIɔ
cJɔ cJɔ cJɔ cJɔ cJɔ cJɔ cJɔ cJɔ cJɔ cJɔ cJɔ cJɔ cJɔ cJɔ cJɔ cJɔ cJɔ cJɔ cJɔ cJɔ
cKɔ cKɔ cKɔ cKɔ cKɔ cKɔ cKɔ cKɔ cKɔ cKɔ cKɔ cKɔ cKɔ cKɔ cKɔ cKɔ cKɔ cKɔ cKɔ cKɔ
cLɔ cLɔ cLɔ cLɔ cLɔ cLɔ cLɔ cLɔ cLɔ cLɔ cLɔ cLɔ cLɔ cLɔ cLɔ cLɔ cLɔ cLɔ cLɔ cLɔ
cMɔ cMɔ cMɔ cMɔ cMɔ cMɔ cMɔ cMɔ cMɔ cMɔ cMɔ cMɔ cMɔ cMɔ cMɔ cMɔ cMɔ cMɔ cMɔ cMɔ
cNɔ cNɔ cNɔ cNɔ cNɔ cNɔ cNɔ cNɔ cNɔ cNɔ cNɔ cNɔ cNɔ cNɔ cNɔ cNɔ cNɔ cNɔ cNɔ cNɔ
cOɔ cOɔ cOɔ cOɔ cOɔ cOɔ cOɔ cOɔ cOɔ cOɔ cOɔ cOɔ cOɔ cOɔ cOɔ cOɔ cOɔ cOɔ cOɔ cOɔ
cPɔ cPɔ cPɔ cPɔ cPɔ cPɔ cPɔ cPɔ cPɔ cPɔ cPɔ cPɔ cPɔ cPɔ cPɔ cPɔ cPɔ cPɔ cPɔ cPɔ
cQɔ cQɔ cQɔ cQɔ cQɔ cQɔ cQɔ cQɔ cQɔ cQɔ cQɔ cQɔ cQɔ cQɔ cQɔ cQɔ cQɔ cQɔ cQɔ cQɔ
cRɔ cRɔ cRɔ cRɔ cRɔ cRɔ cRɔ cRɔ cRɔ cRɔ cRɔ cRɔ cRɔ cRɔ cRɔ cRɔ cRɔ cRɔ cRɔ cRɔ
cSɔ cSɔ cSɔ cSɔ cSɔ cSɔ cSɔ cSɔ cSɔ cSɔ cSɔ cSɔ cSɔ cSɔ cSɔ cSɔ cSɔ cSɔ cSɔ cSɔ
cTɔ cTɔ cTɔ cTɔ cTɔ cTɔ cTɔ cTɔ cTɔ cTɔ cTɔ cTɔ cTɔ cTɔ cTɔ cTɔ cTɔ cTɔ cTɔ cTɔ
cUɔ cUɔ cUɔ cUɔ cUɔ cUɔ cUɔ cUɔ cUɔ cUɔ cUɔ cUɔ cUɔ cUɔ cUɔ cUɔ cUɔ cUɔ cUɔ cUɔ
cVɔ cVɔ cVɔ cVɔ cVɔ cVɔ cVɔ cVɔ cVɔ cVɔ cVɔ cVɔ cVɔ cVɔ cVɔ cVɔ cVɔ cVɔ cVɔ cVɔ
cWɔ cWɔ cWɔ cWɔ cWɔ cWɔ cWɔ cWɔ cWɔ cWɔ cWɔ cWɔ cWɔ cWɔ cWɔ cWɔ cWɔ cWɔ cWɔ cWɔ
cXɔ cXɔ cXɔ cXɔ cXɔ cXɔ cXɔ cXɔ cXɔ cXɔ cXɔ cXɔ cXɔ cXɔ cXɔ cXɔ cXɔ cXɔ cXɔ cXɔ
cYɔ cYɔ cYɔ cYɔ cYɔ cYɔ cYɔ cYɔ cYɔ cYɔ cYɔ cYɔ cYɔ cYɔ cYɔ cYɔ cYɔ cYɔ cYɔ cYɔ
cZɔ cZɔ cZɔ cZɔ cZɔ cZɔ cZɔ cZɔ cZɔ cZɔ cZɔ cZɔ cZɔ cZɔ cZɔ cZɔ cZɔ cZɔ cZɔ cZɔ

CANDIDATE NUMBER | SUBJECT CODE

c0ɔ c0ɔ c0ɔ c0ɔ c0ɔ c0ɔ c0ɔ c0ɔ   c0ɔ c0ɔ c0ɔ
c1ɔ c1ɔ c1ɔ c1ɔ c1ɔ c1ɔ c1ɔ c1ɔ   c1ɔ c1ɔ c1ɔ
c2ɔ c2ɔ c2ɔ c2ɔ c2ɔ c2ɔ c2ɔ c2ɔ   c2ɔ c2ɔ c2ɔ
c3ɔ c3ɔ c3ɔ c3ɔ c3ɔ c3ɔ c3ɔ c3ɔ   c3ɔ c3ɔ c3ɔ
c4ɔ c4ɔ c4ɔ c4ɔ c4ɔ c4ɔ c4ɔ c4ɔ   c4ɔ c4ɔ c4ɔ
c5ɔ c5ɔ c5ɔ c5ɔ c5ɔ c5ɔ c5ɔ c5ɔ   c5ɔ c5ɔ c5ɔ
c6ɔ c6ɔ c6ɔ c6ɔ c6ɔ c6ɔ c6ɔ c6ɔ   c6ɔ c6ɔ c6ɔ
c7ɔ c7ɔ c7ɔ c7ɔ c7ɔ c7ɔ c7ɔ c7ɔ   c7ɔ c7ɔ c7ɔ
c8ɔ c8ɔ c8ɔ c8ɔ c8ɔ c8ɔ c8ɔ c8ɔ   c8ɔ c8ɔ c8ɔ
c9ɔ c9ɔ c9ɔ c9ɔ c9ɔ c9ɔ c9ɔ c9ɔ   c9ɔ c9ɔ c9ɔ

Use HB Pencil to complete this form.

1	cAɔ cBɔ cCɔ cDɔ cEɔ	31	cAɔ cBɔ cCɔ cDɔ cEɔ	61	cAɔ cBɔ cCɔ cDɔ cEɔ	91	cAɔ cBɔ cCɔ cDɔ cEɔ
2	cAɔ cBɔ cCɔ cDɔ cEɔ	32	cAɔ cBɔ cCɔ cDɔ cEɔ	62	cAɔ cBɔ cCɔ cDɔ cEɔ	92	cAɔ cBɔ cCɔ cDɔ cEɔ
3	cAɔ cBɔ cCɔ cDɔ cEɔ	33	cAɔ cBɔ cCɔ cDɔ cEɔ	63	cAɔ cBɔ cCɔ cDɔ cEɔ	93	cAɔ cBɔ cCɔ cDɔ cEɔ
4	cAɔ cBɔ cCɔ cDɔ cEɔ	34	cAɔ cBɔ cCɔ cDɔ cEɔ	64	cAɔ cBɔ cCɔ cDɔ cEɔ	94	cAɔ cBɔ cCɔ cDɔ cEɔ
5	cAɔ cBɔ cCɔ cDɔ cEɔ	35	cAɔ cBɔ cCɔ cDɔ cEɔ	65	cAɔ cBɔ cCɔ cDɔ cEɔ	95	cAɔ cBɔ cCɔ cDɔ cEɔ
6	cAɔ cBɔ cCɔ cDɔ cEɔ	36	cAɔ cBɔ cCɔ cDɔ cEɔ	66	cAɔ cBɔ cCɔ cDɔ cEɔ	96	cAɔ cBɔ cCɔ cDɔ cEɔ
7	cAɔ cBɔ cCɔ cDɔ cEɔ	37	cAɔ cBɔ cCɔ cDɔ cEɔ	67	cAɔ cBɔ cCɔ cDɔ cEɔ	97	cAɔ cBɔ cCɔ cDɔ cEɔ
8	cAɔ cBɔ cCɔ cDɔ cEɔ	38	cAɔ cBɔ cCɔ cDɔ cEɔ	68	cAɔ cBɔ cCɔ cDɔ cEɔ	98	cAɔ cBɔ cCɔ cDɔ cEɔ
9	cAɔ cBɔ cCɔ cDɔ cEɔ	39	cAɔ cBɔ cCɔ cDɔ cEɔ	69	cAɔ cBɔ cCɔ cDɔ cEɔ	99	cAɔ cBɔ cCɔ cDɔ cEɔ
10	cAɔ cBɔ cCɔ cDɔ cEɔ	40	cAɔ cBɔ cCɔ cDɔ cEɔ	70	cAɔ cBɔ cCɔ cDɔ cEɔ	100	cAɔ cBɔ cCɔ cDɔ cEɔ
11	cAɔ cBɔ cCɔ cDɔ cEɔ	41	cAɔ cBɔ cCɔ cDɔ cEɔ	71	cAɔ cBɔ cCɔ cDɔ cEɔ	101	cAɔ cBɔ cCɔ cDɔ cEɔ
12	cAɔ cBɔ cCɔ cDɔ cEɔ	42	cAɔ cBɔ cCɔ cDɔ cEɔ	72	cAɔ cBɔ cCɔ cDɔ cEɔ	102	cAɔ cBɔ cCɔ cDɔ cEɔ
13	cAɔ cBɔ cCɔ cDɔ cEɔ	43	cAɔ cBɔ cCɔ cDɔ cEɔ	73	cAɔ cBɔ cCɔ cDɔ cEɔ	103	cAɔ cBɔ cCɔ cDɔ cEɔ
14	cAɔ cBɔ cCɔ cDɔ cEɔ	44	cAɔ cBɔ cCɔ cDɔ cEɔ	74	cAɔ cBɔ cCɔ cDɔ cEɔ	104	cAɔ cBɔ cCɔ cDɔ cEɔ
15	cAɔ cBɔ cCɔ cDɔ cEɔ	45	cAɔ cBɔ cCɔ cDɔ cEɔ	75	cAɔ cBɔ cCɔ cDɔ cEɔ	105	cAɔ cBɔ cCɔ cDɔ cEɔ
16	cAɔ cBɔ cCɔ cDɔ cEɔ	46	cAɔ cBɔ cCɔ cDɔ cEɔ	76	cAɔ cBɔ cCɔ cDɔ cEɔ	106	cAɔ cBɔ cCɔ cDɔ cEɔ
17	cAɔ cBɔ cCɔ cDɔ cEɔ	47	cAɔ cBɔ cCɔ cDɔ cEɔ	77	cAɔ cBɔ cCɔ cDɔ cEɔ	107	cAɔ cBɔ cCɔ cDɔ cEɔ
18	cAɔ cBɔ cCɔ cDɔ cEɔ	48	cAɔ cBɔ cCɔ cDɔ cEɔ	78	cAɔ cBɔ cCɔ cDɔ cEɔ	108	cAɔ cBɔ cCɔ cDɔ cEɔ
19	cAɔ cBɔ cCɔ cDɔ cEɔ	49	cAɔ cBɔ cCɔ cDɔ cEɔ	79	cAɔ cBɔ cCɔ cDɔ cEɔ	109	cAɔ cBɔ cCɔ cDɔ cEɔ
20	cAɔ cBɔ cCɔ cDɔ cEɔ	50	cAɔ cBɔ cCɔ cDɔ cEɔ	80	cAɔ cBɔ cCɔ cDɔ cEɔ	110	cAɔ cBɔ cCɔ cDɔ cEɔ
21	cAɔ cBɔ cCɔ cDɔ cEɔ	51	cAɔ cBɔ cCɔ cDɔ cEɔ	81	cAɔ cBɔ cCɔ cDɔ cEɔ	111	cAɔ cBɔ cCɔ cDɔ cEɔ
22	cAɔ cBɔ cCɔ cDɔ cEɔ	52	cAɔ cBɔ cCɔ cDɔ cEɔ	82	cAɔ cBɔ cCɔ cDɔ cEɔ	112	cAɔ cBɔ cCɔ cDɔ cEɔ
23	cAɔ cBɔ cCɔ cDɔ cEɔ	53	cAɔ cBɔ cCɔ cDɔ cEɔ	83	cAɔ cBɔ cCɔ cDɔ cEɔ	113	cAɔ cBɔ cCɔ cDɔ cEɔ
24	cAɔ cBɔ cCɔ cDɔ cEɔ	54	cAɔ cBɔ cCɔ cDɔ cEɔ	84	cAɔ cBɔ cCɔ cDɔ cEɔ	114	cAɔ cBɔ cCɔ cDɔ cEɔ
25	cAɔ cBɔ cCɔ cDɔ cEɔ	55	cAɔ cBɔ cCɔ cDɔ cEɔ	85	cAɔ cBɔ cCɔ cDɔ cEɔ	115	cAɔ cBɔ cCɔ cDɔ cEɔ
26	cAɔ cBɔ cCɔ cDɔ cEɔ	56	cAɔ cBɔ cCɔ cDɔ cEɔ	86	cAɔ cBɔ cCɔ cDɔ cEɔ	116	cAɔ cBɔ cCɔ cDɔ cEɔ
27	cAɔ cBɔ cCɔ cDɔ cEɔ	57	cAɔ cBɔ cCɔ cDɔ cEɔ	87	cAɔ cBɔ cCɔ cDɔ cEɔ	117	cAɔ cBɔ cCɔ cDɔ cEɔ
28	cAɔ cBɔ cCɔ cDɔ cEɔ	58	cAɔ cBɔ cCɔ cDɔ cEɔ	88	cAɔ cBɔ cCɔ cDɔ cEɔ	118	cAɔ cBɔ cCɔ cDɔ cEɔ
29	cAɔ cBɔ cCɔ cDɔ cEɔ	59	cAɔ cBɔ cCɔ cDɔ cEɔ	89	cAɔ cBɔ cCɔ cDɔ cEɔ	119	cAɔ cBɔ cCɔ cDɔ cEɔ
30	cAɔ cBɔ cCɔ cDɔ cEɔ	60	cAɔ cBɔ cCɔ cDɔ cEɔ	90	cAɔ cBɔ cCɔ cDɔ cEɔ	120	cAɔ cBɔ cCɔ cDɔ cEɔ

Instant questionnaire 6

Getting students to give you feedback about your teaching need not be a time-consuming process, either for you or for them. The instant questionnaire takes just a few minutes of the lecture or seminar time and has the important advantage that it can address immediate issues.

To write an instant questionnaire, you need to identify the key questions you want to ask about the session and present them in the form of short statements written from the students' point of view, e.g.

a   I need a tutorial on this topic.

b   I could now solve problems of the form ....

c   The explanations were too fast for me.

d   The explanations assumed too much prior knowledge.

Display the statements on the overhead projector and say to the students, 'Please take a piece of paper and write down the question numbers, a to d. Next to each question number write down a rating using the following scale:

    1 = strongly agree

    2 = agree

    3 = neutral or don't know

    4 = disagree

    5 = strongly disagree

Don't sign your paper or give me any other way of identifying who wrote what. Please leave your piece of paper on my desk as you leave the class'. A student's response might then look like this:

    a   1

    b   4

    c   2

    d   2

Because only a limited number of statements is used, the collation of the data can be quick and easy. If, however, collation is a problem due to large student numbers then a standard printed response sheet and an optical mark reader can be used **(see 5 Computer-aided questionnaires)**.

It is easy to report back to students by adding the results to the same overhead projector transparency and showing it to them at the start of the next session.

Students become used to instant questionnaires very quickly and you can then dispense with the overhead projector and simply read out your statements, or even make them up on the spot.

Course content questionnaire

It is common for teachers, when designing courses, to focus their attention on content: they are principally concerned with deciding which topics to include and how much emphasis to give to each. So it makes sense, when the time comes to evaluate a course, to check whether these decisions are in tune with students' needs.

The questionnaire which follows is designed to evaluate course content. It is based on *The pragmatic course evaluation questionnaire*, developed by Martin Haigh, Oxford Polytechnic[1]. The main components of a course are listed in the left-hand column, and students are asked to indicate whether each component should be expanded, retained, reduced or dropped. They are also asked to judge the components according to clarity of purpose and enjoyment.

If you want to use or devise such a questionnaire, these notes may be helpful.

a   It is important to label course components using a form of words which your students will recognise.

b   It can be useful to include on the questionnaire a space to allow students to explain their ratings. This is because they sometimes want course components expanded or dropped for reasons which teachers might not think valid; for example, because they find them easy or difficult.

c   There may of course be good academic reasons for retaining topics which students want you to drop but such a reaction from them might at least indicate a need for changes in the way the topic was taught.

d   It is important to give students an explanation when you are unable to respond to their feedback if, for example, you are constrained by an externally set syllabus or exam. Otherwise they will stop taking your feedback questionnaires seriously.

1   G Gibbs and M Haigh,   *A compendium of course evaluation questionnaires,*
Standing Conference on Educational Development, Birmingham, 1984

Course content questionnaire

Please advise on which topics should be expanded, retained, reduced or dropped. Please also indicate which topics you found more or less enjoyable than average and which topics you couldn't see a clear purpose for. Please add comments which will help me to understand your responses.

Your Advice

	Expand y/n	Retain y/n	Reduce y/n	Drop y/n	Purpose clear y/n	Enjoyed more (+) or less (-) than average +/-	Comments
Lecture 1 on							
Seminar 1 on							
Lectures 2 - 5 on							
Seminar 2 on							
Practical 1 on							
Practical 2 on							
Field trip to							
etc							

Course objectives questionnaire 8

One conclusion which can be drawn from the mass of research literature on students' ratings of their teachers is that there is only a modest relationship between how good students think the teacher is and how well the students do. Apparently questionnaires don't always address important issues. Certainly the trivial aspects of lecturing behaviour which are the focus of some feedback questionnaires seem to have relatively little to do with the quality of student learning. An alternative to this sometimes excessive attention to classroom performance has been to focus instead on course objectives.

An interesting example of such a questionnaire is that developed by David Boud of the University of New South Wales. It examines the congruence between the students' aspirations, the course objectives, learning outcomes and assessment. Such a questionnaire is of use primarily with courses which have clearly specified objectives and so may be of particular value to B/TEC courses.

The questionnaire which follows illustrates this method in the context of a geology course. It shows the response of one student in order to illustrate how far a student's perceptions of a course may vary from what was intended.

It is important with this, as with other questionnaires, to look at individual students' responses as well as to collate the average response of a class. Individual patterns are likely to vary considerably and averaged data could obscure such patterns.

Course objectives questionnaire

To what extent are the course objectives:

(5 = very much so, 1 = not at all!)

Course objectives	objectives of an ideal course	objectives of this course	achieved on this course	likely to be examined
1 Recognise certain rock sequences	5	3	4	1
2 Explain the causes of these rock sequences	4	3	3	1
3 Evaluate alternative explanations	2	4	2	5
4 Explain methodological problems of such evaluations	1	5	1	5

Please add your comments here:

I've got my work cut out, just recognising the rock formations. You see, I'm new to this subject. I know Doctor Granite is into all this alternative theories stuff but it's way over my head. But I bet that's what the exam's about.

Comparative questionnaire 9

Teachers often find that they want to make comparisons between course elements. This may be because they need to track down a problem which has been thrown up by a general questionnaire or simply because they are interested in getting a comparative picture of a whole course.

One way of doing this is to use the same questionnaire across all course elements so as to be able to compare ratings and make relative judgements. The questionnaires featured in items **1** and **5** can be used in this way. Care must be exercised in interpreting these comparisons, however, because it is known that student ratings vary with the type of course, independently of quality. For example first year compulsory courses on methodology or statistics tend to be rated lower than other courses, whoever teaches them and however well they are taught. Ratings also vary according to how and when the questionnaire is administered; for example, before or after an unexpectedly difficult exam.

The main difficulty with using such questionnaires in a comparative way is that students are not being asked to make comparisons but are making absolute judgements about one course element at a time. The results will be more useful if you ask them to make comparisons between course elements.

The most direct way of doing this is to list all the course elements and ask students to rank them according to a particular criterion. For example, students could be asked to give a ranking of 1 to the element they found most interesting, a ranking of 2 to the next most interesting, and so on. You should, however, avoid using criteria which are too broad; for example, if you ask students to rank elements 'in order of importance' you may have difficulty interpreting the rankings which emerge.

Another way is to ask students to make a limited number of ratings of all the course elements. The following questionnaire illustrates this. (It was devised to investigate the issue of inequality of demand between modules which were supposed to be equal.)

Comparison of first year modules

For each module that you have taken please tick a box in :

column 1 to indicate how heavy or light the workload was *in relation to other modules*

column 2 to indicate how heavy or light the intellectual demands were *in relation to other modules*

column 3 to indicate how heavy or light the coursework demands were *in relation to other modules*

	1 Workload	2 Intellectual demands	3 Coursework demands
	Heavy Average Light	Heavy Average Light	Heavy Average Light
No. Module Title			
8203 Organisms and Environment			
8301 Introduction to Geology			
8302 Rock-forming Minerals			
8303 Understanding Rock Sequences			
8501 Introductory Physics			
8201 Levels and Features of Biological Organisation			

etc.

Course components
questionnaire

Teachers put a lot of effort into the different components which make up a course: the lectures, seminars, tutorials, reading lists, essays, and so on. It is not always clear whether all this effort is directed appropriately. It may be, for example, that you are putting a great deal of time into some components which students do not value highly and giving less attention to others which they find helpful, and which they might find even more helpful if you spent a little longer on them. It can be very useful to ask students to rate just how helpful they find the various components of your course.

Crude 'helpfulness' ratings may, however, be difficult to interpret because students will probably be looking for different kinds of help. It is therefore important to be precise in the wording of the rating scale. For example, you could list all the components of your course and ask students how helpful they found them in enabling them to perform well on the course assessment, or to understand key ideas, or to use their private study time effectively etc.

The course components questionnaire which follows[1] is based on part of a student feedback questionnaire developed at Leicester Polytechnic.

---

1   J L Clarke,   *Student feedback questionnaire,*
                        Centre for Educational Development, Leicester Polytechnic, (undated)

Course components questionnaire

How HELPFUL did you find the following in enabling you to achieve the course objectives?

	very helpful	fairly helpful	not a lot of use	of no use	not included in course	would have been helpful if included
1 Reading lists						
2 Set books						
3 Lecture notes						
4 Lectures						
5 Handouts						
6 Audio-visual aids						
7 Seminars						
8 Tutorials						
9 Problem sessions						
10 Laboratory sessions						
11 Essay(s)						
12 Report writing						
13 Problem sheets						
14 Private reading						
15 Field trip(s)						
16 Visiting lecturer(s)						
17 Demonstrations						
18						
19						
20						

21 Please list any other components which you found helpful, or would have found helpful if they had been included.

....

....

Which issues matter? 11

One of the most common criticisms of questionnaires involving rating scales is that it is likely that some of the questionnaire items concern issues which are not important to students. This is because the items are usually chosen by the teacher, or may even come from a standard questionnaire, and will have been selected from the teacher's perspective. For example it is common for teachers to be more concerned about the 'performance' aspect of their lecturing than are their students. Since students tend to rate every item regardless of how little it matters to them, this difference in the perceived importance of issues is not usually apparent.

This problem can be avoided by involving students in the design of questionnaires in one of the following ways.

a   Interview students in order to identify issues which matter to them, and then incorporate these issues into a questionnaire **(see 15 Interviewing students)**.

b   Check your draft questionnaire with a few students and ask them to delete the items they think are unimportant and to suggest others.

c   Get students to devise questionnaire items themselves **(see 18 Student-devised questionnaires)**.

If you are committed to using a standard questionnaire then you can ask students not just to rate each item, but also to indicate how important it is for them. A student feedback questionnaire developed at North East London Polytechnic in the 70's[1] illustrates this. It consists of a list of 23 standard items (e.g. 'The lecturer is always prepared for his or her classes', 'The lecturer returns written work promptly').

---

1   P S Bradbury and P Ramsden,   'Student evaluation of teaching at North East London Polytechnic' in *Evaluating Teaching in Higher Education*, U T M U, Institute of Education, London,1975

Students show how far they agree or disagree with each statement using the scale:

Strongly Disagree	Disagree	Neither Agree nor Disagree	Agree	Strongly Agree
1	2	3	4	5

The same 23 questionnaire items are then repeated and students are asked: 'Please indicate how important you think it is that lecturers teaching on this course should show each of the following characteristics. Do this by circling the appropriate number on the five point scale'.

Of little importance				Of great importance
1	2	3	4	5

In practice it has been found that students in each subject area have their own characteristic views on which are the important issues.

Checking out your hunches 12

Most teachers have hunches about what is working well, and why. They also tend to act on these hunches and make changes in their teaching, without finding out whether they are correct. Students, however, often have quite different hunches as to why problems are occurring. It is very easy, and also illuminating, to check out whether your hunches are shared by your students.

To do this you need to write down a series of brief statements about what you think is actually taking place on your course. For example you might write down 'The practical write-ups are taking up a lot of students' time' or 'Students seemed not to demonstrate what they knew in the exam; perhaps they revised the wrong things'.

The next stage is to re-write these hunches from the students' point of view. For example, 'The practical work takes too long to write up' or 'The exam did not contain questions about what I knew'.

Alternatively, instead of starting from your own hunches and translating them into student statements, you can start off by trying to guess the kinds of things students would say when they are talking to each other about your course. You may also want to include statements about things which seem to be going well.

These statements are then listed on a questionnaire and students are asked to indicate whether they agree with them or not, using a rating scale. It is probably helpful if the questionnaire mixes positive and negative statements so that students are obliged to think carefully about each one. The results of the questionnaire give you an indication of how far students share your hunches. (Though of course there is still the chance that you are all wrong!)

The questionnaire which follows was designed to check out some hunches which a physics lecturer had about the causes of an unexpectedly high failure rate on one of his courses. Action was taken on the basis of the questionnaire results which greatly reduced the failure rate.

Course evaluation questionnaire

The purpose of this survey is to provide information which will be used to improve the course. The findings will be discussed with the student representatives on the course committee. Please indicate your answers by entering a tick in the appropriate boxes.

		strongly agree	agree	neither agree nor disagree	disagree	strongly disagree
1	The different topics are unrelated to each other	......	......	......	......	......
2	The basic ideas are very difficult to understand	......	......	......	......	......
3	There are too many new ideas to grasp in one term	......	......	......	......	......
4	The practical work takes too long to write up	......	......	......	......	......
5	The practical work does not relate to the lectures	......	......	......	......	......
6	The practical work was necessary to understand some of the lectures	......	......	......	......	......
7	The exam was more difficult than most others	......	......	......	......	......
8	My understanding was helped by my tutorials	......	......	......	......	......
9	My result was what I expected	......	......	......	......	......
10	Only people who did well in the first year could expect to pass this course	......	......	......	......	......
11	Only people who had properly understood the introduction to these topics last term could expect to pass	......	......	......	......	......
12	The exam did not contain questions about what I knew	......	......	......	......	......
13	I would have done better if the non-compulsory part of the exam had contained 4 short questions instead of 2 long ones	......	......	......	......	......
14	I did not find any one topic too hard to understand in itself	......	......	......	......	......
15	I would not have taken this course if it had not been compulsory	......	......	......	......	......

Open-ended questions 13

Open-ended questions are often placed at the bottom of questionnaires which otherwise contain only rating scales and 'tick a box' questions. Typically they ask whether respondents have 'other comments', 'anything to add' etc. It is unusual for such questions to be successful. On the few occasions when they do succeed in eliciting many responses, these are so varied in their focus that they give little overall impression of what students think. They may serve the function of giving scope to students who are frustrated by closed questions, but they seldom produce useful data.

Some forms of open question do work, however, particularly if they are focussed in some way, e.g.

What went well? What went badly?

What were the best things? What were the worst things?

What (if anything) was particularly memorable?

What change(s) would you suggest?

How else might this practical/part of the course/topic have been tackled?

What advice would you give to a student about to start this course?

If you had to choose 25% of the lectures/seminars/course to miss, what would this include?

There are also some tricks of layout which discourage students from writing single-word responses in huge letters so as to fill all the available space as quickly as possible:

a   Add rows of dotted lines after the question to indicate that the space should be filled up, and in small writing, e.g.

What were the best features of the lectures?

....

....

....

....

b   Add numbers to the rows of dotted lines and ask for a specific number of responses, e.g.

*What were the **three** worst things about the teaching?*

1...

....

2...

....

3...

....

c   Ask for explanations for responses, e.g.

List the best features of the laboratory sessions and explain why each was important to you.

Feature   **Explanation**

1................................   ....

                                        ....

                                        ....

                                        ....

2................................   ....

                                        ....

                                        ....

                                        ....

The example which follows illustrates the use of open-ended questions in an appraisal questionnaire.

Feedback form

Course: .... Teacher:...

In the spaces below make a note of up to three things you like about the course.

1 ....

....

2 ....

....

3 ....

....

In the spaces below make a note of up to three suggestions which, for you, would improve the course.

1 ....

....

2 ....

....

3 ....

....

signed ....

date ....

Self-evaluation checklist   14

The self-evaluation checklist which follows[1] is similar in form to a standard student feedback questionnaire. However it is intended to be completed by the teacher. This takes two minutes at the end of a teaching session and involves none of the students' time and no time collating questionnaire data. Because it is so easy and quick to use it could be completed after each of a series of sessions in order to identify areas which might benefit from closer attention. It can also be used to find out whether different courses are taught in different ways, or whether different methods reveal different strengths and weaknesses.

You may well reflect upon your teaching without the use of such a checklist. However a checklist can add finer discrimination to your observations. It can also help in providing a framework to structure reflection, encouraging you to examine aspects of your teaching you might rather ignore, and making it easier to compare your teaching in a range of different situations. You can use it from time to time as a student feedback questionnaire to check out whether your self ratings are similar to the perceptions of students.

This checklist is oriented towards lectures. It would be a simple matter to invent a similar list for seminar or laboratory teaching.

1   Pat Shears,   'Developing a system of appraisal of performance within a college of non-advanced further education', *SRHE Evaluation Newsletter*, 6, 1, 21-30, 1982

Self-evaluation checklist

Record with a tick in the appropriate column the
comments which come closest to your opinion
of your performance in each of the following areas:

	very well	satis- factorily	not very well	poorly	not applicable

How well did I ....?

		very well	satis- factorily	not very well	poorly	not applicable
1	link this session to other sessions	....	....	....	....	....
2	introduce this session	....	....	....	....	....
3	make the aims clear to the students	....	....	....	....	....
4	move clearly from stage to stage	....	....	....	....	....
5	emphasise key points	....	....	....	....	....
6	summarise the session	....	....	....	....	....
7	maintain an appropriate pace	....	....	....	....	....
8	capture students' interest	....	....	....	....	....
9	maintain students' interest	....	....	....	....	....
10	handle problems of inattention	....	....	....	....	....
11	ask questions	....	....	....	....	....
12	handle student questions and responses	....	....	....	....	....
13	direct student tasks	....	....	....	....	....
14	cope with the range of ability	....	....	....	....	....
15	monitor student activity	....	....	....	....	....
16	use aids as illustrations	....	....	....	....	....
17	make contact with all class members	....	....	....	....	....
18	cope with individual difficulties	....	....	....	....	....
19	keep the material relevant	....	....	....	....	....
20	use my voice and body movements	....	....	....	....	....
21	check on student learning	....	....	....	....	....
22	build up student confidence	....	....	....	....	....
23	convey my enthusiasm	....	....	....	....	....
24	provide a model of good practice	....	....	....	....	....

Appraisal using interviews and discussions

Interviewing students 15

Interviewing is a very effective way of determining people's opinions and perceptions; indeed it is one of the methods most commonly used in market research and opinion polls. It also has considerable potential for the appraisal of teaching.

As an appraisal tool, interviewing is generally best used in conjunction with other methods. (If interviews are the sole source of evidence, they will either be impossibly time-consuming or open to criticism for not being rigorous, representative or neutral.)

The following examples illustrate three ways of using interviews as part of the appraisal process.

a   Interviews can be used as the first stage in a questionnaire survey, in order to identify what the main issues are and to keep the subsequent questionnaire to a manageable length. Short interviews with a very few students, analysed only by taking brief notes, may be all that is necessary. Interview questions can be of the type: 'What issues do you think the questionnaire should deal with?' In a sense the questionnaire would then be checking out the extent to which those issues were important to all students.

b   Interviews can be used as a preliminary to discussion. Sometimes it is useful to have rich and hard-hitting evidence to start a debate about how a course is operating and how students experience it. Here it may not matter if selected student quotes are unrepresentative, as long as they are evocative. You might ask, for example, ' What on this course did you really get worked up about?'

c   Interviews can be used as the final stage of a questionnaire survey. They are useful if you want to follow up or supplement the questionnaire in some way. For example, you may have difficulty interpreting the quantitative results. A few quick questions could focus on this, e.g. 'Some students seem to find this course very intellectually demanding, but others find it relatively easy. Why do you think that is?' Or you may want some quotations from students to illustrate your quantitative results, perhaps for a report, in which case you could ask questions to elicit descriptive answers, e.g. 'Most students' response to question 7 was that the practicals took too long to write up. How did you find it?'

It is important to explain carefully to students the purpose and format of the interviews and to reassure them that their contributions, if used, will be quoted anonymously. As interviewer you should say as little as possible and aim to be unobtrusive.

There are a number of general-purpose open-ended questions which will safely guide you through most interviews.

a   Asking for elaboration:
'Can you say a bit more about that?'

b   Asking for a concrete example:
'Can you give me a specific example?'

c   Checking that a comment is not an isolated example:
'Is it always like that?' or 'Can you describe other examples of that happening?'

d   Asking how important an issue is:
'How do you feel about that?'

e   Asking for alternative suggestions:
'How else could that be done?'

f   Using value judgements as a way to start:
'What did you find good/bad about that?'

g   Checking that you understand:
'Let's check that I've got this right. You say that ......?'

Rounds 16

In a round every student has a turn to speak, uninterrupted, on a given topic. The teacher normally joins in too. If the round is being used for appraisal, the topic could be 'What I think of the course so far' or 'A piece of advice that I'd give to a student starting this course'.

The use of rounds prevents confident or aggressive students from doing all the talking and ensures that everyone has an equal chance to contribute. Rounds also tend to foster more interesting and helpful feedback than the impersonal questionnaire, though clearly this is at the expense of some loss of confidentiality.

Rounds are most suitable for small groups: some students find it intimidating to speak in front of more than a dozen people. The feedback will be more focussed if the topic is limited in some way, too, e.g. 'One thing that I like about this course and one suggestion for improvement' or 'One difficulty I've had on this course' or 'One word to describe Monday's lecture'. It is also generally a good idea to keep a record of what people say.

There are ground rules for rounds which should be explained to students before they begin.

a   Speak in turn.

b   It's OK to pass (i.e. if you don't want to contribute to the round, just say 'Pass').

c   It's OK to repeat what someone else has said (i.e. if someone else says what you were going to say yourself, you don't need to think of something different to say, just for the sake of it).

d   Listen to other people's contributions without commenting, either verbally or non-verbally, whether you agree with them or not.

Structured group feedback

One method of appraising your teaching is to hold a meeting with a whole class where you ask the students for feedback. This type of meeting, however, needs to be structured in some way if it is to be useful. An unstructured session is likely to be unrewarding or even unpleasant: there is a danger that the majority of students will not contribute to the discussion and that extreme positions and strongly held minority views will dominate. At best students and teacher may come away unclear about the outcome of the meeting; at worst both may become defensive and resentful.

The exercise which follows gives students the opportunity to contribute to the feedback equally and with a degree of anonymity. It also gives them time to think through their own views before being confronted with other people's. It puts extreme and minority views to the test. It gives the teacher a more neutral role and ensures that the outcome is recorded fully.

The exercise takes 45-60 minutes to run. With a class of more than 50 it could take a little longer. A class of fewer than 12 would need a less formal structure.

Stage 1   Students work alone

Students are asked to make notes about the good and bad features of their course, using the pro forma overleaf. (Sample comments have been written in to illustrate its use.)

Stage 2   Students work in groups of four

One student acts as scribe and records comments agreed by members of the group of four. No comment may be recorded which is not a majority view. (Compromises and re-draftings may be necessary.)

Stage 3 Students work as a whole group

The teacher, or an 'honest broker' **(see 26)**, takes one good point about the course from each group in turn, checks that the majority of the class agrees and then writes it up on the board, going round the groups until no new points emerge. The same process is continued for each of the six cells in the pro forma. The class is then invited to make adjustments to the overall picture which has been built up on the board.

A framework for structured group feedback

	GOOD POINTS	BAD POINTS
About the COURSE		
About the TEACHING		
About us, the STUDENTS		

It is possible to involve all the teachers on a large team-taught course by having them form one of the sub-groups who work together at stage 2 to pool points. It can be effective to fill two blackboards with feedback, the second containing the teachers' comments on the course, on themselves as teachers and on their students. This can then provide a basis for a discussion of the differences and similarities between the students' and teachers' views of the course.

Student-devised questionnaires 18

One of the problems with questionnaires devised by teachers is that they focus on issues which, though they are important to the teacher, may not matter much to the students. It can be very effective to get a student group to devise their own questionnaire, which deals with issues which are of central concern to them. In the following class-based exercise, the students also rate their own questionnaire and produce collated results within a one-hour session.

Stage 1   Before the session, decide which areas of your teaching you want students to appraise. These areas should be sufficiently broadly defined to help students to focus their thoughts without constraining them. Four or five areas will be enough, e.g. assessment, lectures, seminars, practicals, content. Let students know what these are in advance.

Write the names of the four or five areas on separate poster-sized sheets of paper, to act as headings large enough to be read across the room. Get together a large number of file cards or small pieces of paper, drawing pins, Sellotape or Blu-Tack (depending on the walls or notice-boards available), half a dozen A3 or A2 sheets and some felt tip pens.

Stage 2   Pin up the posters so that everyone can see them.

Introduce the session to the students. The following points should encourage them to participate.

a   Evaluation is important and students have a responsibility to help improve courses.

b   Everyone will have the opportunity to contribute.

c   All feedback will be anonymous.

Stage 3   Ask students, working on their own, to write the poster headings on a sheet of paper and to write comments under each heading.

Stage 4   Ask students to form groups and assign one group to each of the posters. (If there are more than 30 students this may result in groups of more than six, in which case the groups can be sub-divided.) Give each group plenty of file cards. Ask the students to write statements about the area of teaching indicated on their poster and to pin them up on the poster under the heading. (The group doesn't have to agree about the statements at this stage.) The file cards should be displayed as soon as they are written, and students should be encouraged to go and see what other groups have pinned up on the other posters. (This active to-ing and fro-ing helps to keep students alert.)

Stage 5   When the students have finished writing and pinning up their statements, each group rotates to the next poster. Their task is then to reduce the many statements which they find there to half a dozen with which they can agree or disagree. (Minority issues which drop out at this stage are not lost, as you can read all the individual file cards afterwards.) You may need to suggest that students avoid statements with negatives, alternatives or other complications which do not lend themselves to the agree/disagree treatment. The half-dozen statements should then be written out on a fresh poster in the form of a questionnaire with a five-point rating scale alongside each statement. If you give the students a pro forma to copy, this will ensure that all the questionnaires have the same format.

Statement	strongly agree	agree	neutral	disagree	strongly disagree
1	......	......	......	......	......
2	......	......	......	......	......
etc.					

Stage 6 Ask students to go round the posters and individually rate each statement by ticking the appropriate box. The following chart shows the results of a student-devised questionnaire on a philosophy of education course.

Statement	strongly agree	agree	neutral	disagree	strongly disagree
1 Small seminars are a good idea	18	2	0	0	0
2 More handouts wanted	18	2	0	0	0
3 Seminars are a bit erratic	6	2	0	2	10
4 I like Rousseau and Marx as main authors	6	4	4	2	4
5 Discussion file is too much work	2	2	6	6	4
6 Seminars should be more highly structured	4	8	0	6	2

Stage 7 Encourage the whole class to discuss the pooled results. You can also ask for clarification and elaboration.

(This item was written with the help of Morwena Griffiths, Oxford Polytechnic.)

Nominal Group Technique

19

Nominal Group Technique (NGT)[1] is a technique for generating ideas in groups and reflecting on them. It is similar to brainstorming in that it initially involves recording ideas without evaluating them, but it is more highly structured and specifically addresses itself to subsequent action.

NGT is particularly useful when your starting point in a discussion is the feelings and experiences of the group as, for example, the reactions of a group of students to a course. The technique brings out these initial unanalysed reactions and then provides a framework for organising and analysing them. It has much more chance of success than the unstructured discussion which starts with the question, 'Well, what did you think of the course this year, then?'

An NGT meeting normally involves eight stages:

1 **Asking the question**

2 **Writing individual responses**

3 **Listing the responses**

4 **Clarifying the responses**

5 **Evaluating and ranking the responses**

6 **Discussion**

7 **Plenary**

8 **Planning ahead**

1 **Asking the question**

The students are presented with a question. This can be fairly general (e.g. 'What changes need to be made to this course?') or specific (e.g. 'What difficulties have

---

1   A L Delbecq, A H Van de Ven   *Group techniques for program planning: a guide to Nominal*
    and D H Gustafson,   *and Delphi Processes*, Scott, Foresman, 1975

you experienced in the organic chemistry practicals?') or personal (e.g. 'How do you feel you have developed as a person on the course so far?')

2 Writing individual responses

Individuals are asked to write down their own responses to the set question, and then to rank them in order of importance. About ten minutes is allowed for this. Announce how much time is to be allowed so that students can pace themselves and work at an appropriate level of detail. Discussion is not permitted. Responses which seem trivial should not be omitted as the intention is to generate as much material as possible; analysis will take place later.

3 Listing the responses

Participants form groups of 8-10 people. Each group needs a neutral 'leader' whose role will be to co-ordinate the work of the group; this role could be performed by an 'honest broker' **(see 26)**. Groups pool their responses to form a composite list. The leader writes the list on a board or flipchart. At this stage the items are not commented upon, criticised or edited in any way. Individuals may be influenced by other people's contributions to make additional suggestions of their own, but this should not develop into a discussion. The aim is to draw up as large a list as possible, involving all members of the group. This may take up to three-quarters of an hour.

4 Clarifying the responses

In stage 3 the responses were not explained. In stage 4 the leader takes the group through the listed responses making sure that everyone understands what they all mean. Again no discussion or criticism of the items is permitted.

5 Evaluating and ranking the responses

The purpose at this stage is to rank the items on the list. A voting system can be used. Criteria such as urgency, interest, personal concern and so on should be agreed and each item rated on a 1-5 scale according to each of the criteria (1 = least urgent, 5 = most urgent). Students can be limited to five votes altogether, to speed the process. Adding up the ratings for each item will give a crude indication of the group's perception of the list. It is intended that evaluation through discussion does not take place until this overall picture emerges.

6 Discussion

Now that the students in the group can see which responses are generally considered important, more open discussion can take place. Useful questions to move along such a discussion include 'What strikes you as interesting?' or 'What suprises you by its omission?'

7 Plenary

At this stage the separate groups come together and the ranked lists of responses are pooled. The top ten from each group, for example, can be put together. Overlapping items can be combined or more carefully discriminated and a second voting procedure operated. The outcome is an overall ranking of the key responses so that it is quite clear what the important issues are.

8 Planning ahead

Students can also be encouraged to discuss possible changes in the course and in teaching, once the key issues are clear.

(This item was written with the help of Mike O'Neil, Trent Polytechnic.)

Group self-appraisal

20

While many forms of teaching depend largely upon the teacher for their success, group projects rely heavily on the input and interaction of the students. It is appropriate therefore that students in such a group conduct an appraisal of their own operation. This not only encourages them to improve their effectiveness as a group but can also contribute to the teacher's appraisal of the course.

Students can find it difficult to discuss their own and each other's behaviour, so two self-appraisal sheets are offered here to help initiate discussion. Students can either complete the sheets individually, and then pool and compare responses in the group, or the whole group can discuss each question in turn before making a group response. Once these issues have been raised in this way an appraisal discussion will be much easier to handle.

It will probably be better if the students have this discussion without you. You could come in at the end and ask them to report to you.

The self-appraisal sheet which follows is based on a similar checklist in *The Small Group Tutorial*, McMaster University Education Monograph, 3, 1972.

Group self-appraisal sheet

		Always				Never

About the group:

1	All members of the group attend regularly	....	....	....	....	....
2	All members of the group arrive promptly	....	....	....	....	....
3	The group has responded to the feelings or moods expressed by its members	....	....	....	....	....
4	The group has listened to and responded to members' ideas and comments	....	....	....	....	....
5	All members of the group are involved and have participated in discussion	....	....	....	....	....
6	The atmosphere in the group has been friendly and open	....	....	....	....	....
7	The group has confronted any member who was hindering the group (e.g. by undue arguing, straying off the topic, telling anecdotes)	....	....	....	....	....
8	The group has discussed areas of conflict rather than avoiding conflict or allowing it to become destructive	....	....	....	....	....
9	The group has discussed its progress at the end of meetings	....	....	....	....	....
10	At the end of meetings the group has set itself clear tasks for its next meeting	....	....	....	....	....

About the tutor:

11	The tutor encourages discussion before presenting his/her own ideas	....	....	....	....	....
12	The tutor synthesises and summarises the discussion before moving on to the next topic	....	....	....	....	....
13	The tutor asks the group before moving on to the next topic	....	....	....	....	....
14	The tutor does not dominate	....	....	....	....	....

Project group self-appraisal sheet

1 Degree of mutual trust

High trust	2	1	0	1	2	High suspicion

2 Degree of mutual support

Genuine support for each other	2	1	0	1	2	Everyone for themselves

3 Communications

Open, honest	2	1	0	1	2	Guarded, cautious

4 Group objectives

Clearly understood by group	2	1	0	1	2	Not understood by group
Group is committed to objectives	2	1	0	1	2	Group is negative towards objectives
High achievement of objectives	2	1	0	1	2	Low achievement of objectives

5 Handling conflicts within the group

We face up to conflicts and work through them	2	1	0	1	2	We deny, avoid or suppress conflicts

6 Utilisation of group resources

My ideas, abilities, knowledge & experience are properly used	2	1	0	1	2	My ideas, abilities, knowledge & experience are not properly used
Others' ideas, abilities, knowledge & experience are properly used	2	1	0	1	2	Others' ideas, abilities, knowledge & experience are not properly used

7 Suitability of group method

The way the group works is suitable for our objectives	2	1	0	1	2	The way the group works is not suitable for our objectives

Other comments:

Long-term appraisal 21

As well as appraising your courses while they are running, and as they are finishing, you may also want some feedback from your students about the long-term benefits which your teaching has had on them. Long-term appraisal is particularly important in the case of vocational courses where the usefulness and relevance of what they learned in college may be clear to students only when they have been working for some time in the field. Non-vocational courses too, however, can benefit from being evaluated by students who have had time to reflect on what they have learned.

You can carry out long-term appraisal by sending all your students a questionnaire or you may be able to invite them back to college for an appraisal workshop, which could be linked to a refresher course or a reunion. In many ways a workshop is preferable to a questionnaire because it gives the opportunity for discussions and interviews as well as written feedback. In either case you need to be clear about what questions you want to ask. Some suggestions follow.

for a non-vocational course

Which part(s) of the course do you remember most clearly? Why?
Which part(s) of the course have been most useful to you since you left?
How could the course have been improved?

for a vocational course

Which part(s) of the course have been most useful to you in your job?
Which part(s) of the course have been least useful to you in your job?
Can you think of any way(s) in which the course could be made more relevant to your job?

for an in-service course

How have you changed since the course?

What new things have you done in your job since the course?

What old things have you done differently?

What aspects of your job do you still not feel confident about?

(This item was written with the help of Linda Ewles, Senior Health Education Officer, Bristol.)

Appraisal using video and audio recordings

2 2   Vox pop

2 3   Student-made videos

2 4   Microteaching

2 5   Interpersonal Process Recall

Vox pop 22

An informal and often lively appraisal of teaching can be obtained by producing a short *vox pop* video or audio recording of student views in much the same way as broadcasting crews sample the views of passers-by in the street. *Vox pop* is not research data. The views expressed are not balanced, or even always sensible. But such a recording never fails to raise teachers' awareness of the fact that students see a lot of teaching and they know what they like.

When we made a *vox pop* video at Bristol Polytechnic, it took an interviewer and a two-person crew about four hours, including two hours' editing time, to interview students and produce a stimulating fifteen-minute video from the material which was filmed. This video has been used by at least twenty different groups of teachers.

If you want to make a *vox pop* video, your educational services unit may help with equipment and provide a camera crew. All you need to do is stand outside the student union shop or cafe and ask passers-by if they would be prepared to answer a few questions. Most people will not refuse.

You will save yourself a lot of editing time later if you use a short list of questions and ask them in the same order for each interview. The list which follows shows the questions used for the Bristol Polytechnic *vox pop* video on lectures.

THE QUESTIONS

Lectures

1 What happens in your lectures?

2 What's the worst thing that happens in your lectures?

3 What do you **do** in the lecture?

4 What do you think the lecturer is trying to do in the lecture?

5 What does the lecturer think **you're** doing in the lecture?

Notes

1 How do you know when the lecturer is saying something important?

2 What do you do with the notes you take?

3 How do you know if you've got it down right?

4 Does the lecturer ever check up on what you're doing?

Finishing off

1 If you could give your lecturers one piece of advice what would it be?

2 If you came out of a lecture thinking 'That was a really good lecture' what would it have been like?

Editing simply involves selecting the most illuminating answers to each of the questions. In selecting items to include, aim for impact rather than balance.

Show your *vox pop* video to your colleagues at a departmental meeting, or to your own students. If colleagues are sceptical about the general validity of the comments made use one of the questionnaires in the earlier part of this book to check them out.

Student-made videos 23

Showing a video of students' views is an intimate and colourful way of presenting a review of a course **(see 22 *Vox pop)*.** If the video is made by the students themselves it also offers a particularly student-focussed appraisal: as with student-devised questionnaires **(see 18)**, the questions are being asked, as well as answered, by the students.

If your students are learning media skills as part of their course, you can expect them to be able to film and edit their own video. Otherwise they will probably need some practical help, either from you or from your educational services unit, though the technical quality of the video need not be an issue. Either way, they are likely to find the experience rewarding and enjoyable.

A student group at Newcastle Polytechnic made a video about their course. The group decided on a series of topic headings, e.g. lectures, project support, accommodation. Each student was allocated an equal amount of time to speak to the camera on any of these topics. The material was edited by one of the students and the final production was checked by the whole group for accuracy and balance. The tape was then given to the course team and was used by them as an integral part of the appraisal procedure at the end of the year. It was also shown to the course management committee, the examination board and the external examiners.

Microteaching 24

Microteaching is the name given to a method of teacher training which involves identifying specific teaching skills, making a videotape recording of a short teaching session and then giving the trainee teacher detailed feedback. It is generally followed by a second recording in which the trainee teacher repeats the session and tries to put the feedback into practice. In contrast with Interpersonal Process Recall **(see 25)**, microteaching concentrates on observable behaviour rather than on perceptions and feelings. It also, as its name implies, operates at a micro rather than a macro level.

To some extent microteaching in its strictest form has fallen out of favour as it is thought that the minutiae of teachers' behaviour may be less important than broader strategic, social and emotional issues. However, as a way of getting detailed and specific feedback on an aspect of your teaching which concerns you, microteaching remains a useful technique.

If you want to use this technique to appraise your own teaching, you first need to decide what you will focus on. The following lists come from a microteaching course run at Lancaster University and illustrate the kind of teaching behaviour which microteaching commonly explores.

a   Habits discouraged by the course
Asking 'yes' or 'no' questions
Repeating questions
Answering own questions
Punitive response to wrong answers

b Skills encouraged by the course

Prompting

Higher order questioning

Asking for sets of related facts

Seeking clarification

Redirection

Refocussing

Pausing

Calling on non-volunteers

The staff of your educational development unit will record one of your teaching sessions and will also help you with feedback if requested. Alternatively, micro teaching can be run by pairs or groups of teachers who give each other feedback.

Reference

E Perrot,   *Microteaching in higher education,* Research into Higher Education Monograph 31 Society for Research into Higher Education, Guildford, 1977

Interpersonal Process Recall 25

Interpersonal Process Recall (IPR) is a technique which enables people who have been involved in a human interaction to recall later the thoughts and feelings they had and to learn from them. It uses a video recording of the event to prompt the recall and a particular method of questioning to facilitate the learning. IPR can offer teachers an opportunity to appraise their teaching, provide feedback from students, and enable groups to reflect on their ways of working.

If you want to use IPR to reflect on your teaching, you need to record one of your lectures or classes and then sit down with a colleague to analyse the videotape. When you recall something of significance, prompted by the recording, stop the tape. (With IPR it is important that the control is in the hands of the person who has been videotaped.) The role of your colleague is not to make judgements or give advice but to ask non-directive questions which take the reflection further than it might otherwise go. Useful questions include:

    What was going on then?
    How did you feel at that point? Have you felt like that before?
    What were you thinking?
    How were the students feeling and what were they thinking?
    What else could you have done at that point? What stopped you?
    If you had done that, how would it have felt?
    Have you felt like that before? Tell me about that time.
    What would you have liked to say to the students at that point?
    What would they have liked you to have done?
    What did you want to happen?
    What do you think the students wanted to happen?
    What did you want the students to say?
    Was there any risk for you?
    Were there any risks for the students?

If you want to use IPR to get feedback from students, there is a three-stage process you can follow. First, your colleague sits down either with individual students, or with a whole seminar or even a lecture group, and plays the video through, asking the students to call out and stop it when they have something to say. This takes place in your absence so that students can talk freely about their thoughts and feelings. Secondly, your colleague goes through the same process with you in the absence of the students. And thirdly, you and the students can then view the video together, both parties choosing where to stop the tape. It is important that your colleague again controls the question and answer process so that the session does not degenerate into an informal chat, or a slanging match.

IPR has been used extensively to help groups who work together regularly, such as departmental committees, research groups, student project groups, supervisors and students, and so on. Its strength lies in its ability to reveal those things which are normally suppressed and kept private, and to tackle these in a controlled and non-threatening way, without the need for sophisticated facilitative or counselling skills.

The method works so well that if video is not available, or would be too intrusive, an audio tape can usually serve as a substitute. With both video and audiotape, however, the vividness and detail fade with time, and the recall session should take place within 24 hours of the original recording if possible.

Training courses in the use of IPR are run by Professor Norman Kagan, University of Houston, who is the founder of the method, and by *I P R Associates, c/o Educational Methods Unit, Oxford Polytechnic.*

(This item was written with the help of David Jaques, Oxford Polytechnic.)

Reference

P Marland,   'Stimulated Recall from Video' in O. Zuber-Skerritt (Ed.),
              Video in Higher Education, Kogan Page, 1984

Appraisal with help from colleagues

Honest broker

Students are often reluctant to give their teachers direct feedback, usually because they are afraid of the effect it may have on their marks. In such a situation it can be useful to have a neutral outsider involved in the appraisal of teaching. This 'honest broker' could be a colleague from another department or someone from an educational development unit, but in any case should be unconnected with the course the students are studying, and should be perceived by both the teacher and the students as having no particular axe to grind, and as acting on behalf of the teacher, rather than on behalf of a superior such as a head of department. The main qualifications of an honest broker are honesty and neutrality rather than any specific expertise.

An honest broker can be used to chair appraisal discussions, analyse questionnaire data, interview students or review video recordings. This can be done on a regular basis or in response to particular issues which the teacher wants to investigate. Two teachers can also act as honest broker for one another.

It is essential that the person selected agrees to complete confidentiality, and hands over to the teacher the ownership of any data collected.

Debriefing with a colleague 27

Simply talking things over with a colleague after a teaching session can be useful as a way of appraising your own teaching in an informal way. (And it may be more obviously useful if the two of you have taught the session together.) But the conventions of everyday conversation usually limit the value that such a chat can have: there is not likely to be the opportunity to explore and analyse the session in depth.

It is a simple matter to introduce a few rules to make the debriefing more productive than is generally the case in a conversation.

a   **Share the time**

If the participants have equal time to speak, this puts the appraisal on a firm basis of fairness and reciprocity. The length of time can be anything from two minutes to an hour.

b   **Listeners keep quiet**

If the listener gives full attention to the speaker but does not speak or intervene in any way, this encourages the speaker to explore things in depth, safe in the knowledge that there will be no interruptions.

c   **Maintain confidentiality**

If the participants know that they are speaking in confidence, there will be a high level of trust which in turn will foster openness.

Principles for giving and receiving feedback

28

The principles listed overleaf are designed to make appraisal between colleagues constructive and realistic and to discourage embarrassment or defensiveness. If they are followed, feedback becomes easier to give and easier to listen to, accept and act upon. If you were to ask a colleague to offer critical feedback on your teaching, then you should find it helpful if you both read through these principles at the start of your meeting.

Giving and receiving feedback

Giving feedback

a   Invite the recipient to speak first. This fosters the skills of self criticism and protects self respect.

b   Be specific rather than general. To be told that one is disorganised will probably not be as useful as to be told: 'When you lost your place during your lecture and couldn't find the right notes I found it distracting'.

c   Balance positive and negative feedback. Positive feedback on its own allows no room for improvement and negative feedback on its own is discouraging.

d   Direct your feedback towards behaviour that your colleague can control. It would not be helpful, for example, to comment on someone's lisp.

e   Ask for confirmation from a third party. For example, if you are giving feedback to your colleague at the end of a seminar and the students are still present, then check out the accuracy of your feedback with them.

Receiving feedback

a   Listen to the feedback without comment. You will hear more if you concentrate on listening rather than explaining or justifying yourself.

b   Ask for clarification at the end. You need to be sure that you understand exactly what your colleague is saying about you and what evidence the comments are based on.

c   Devise action plans. Specify ways in which you want to change, new ideas you want to try etc.

d   Keep a written record. This can be used for later reflection, action planning and appraisal interviews.

A self-appraisal procedure 29

This procedure offers the teacher a formal structure for self-appraisal. It involves individual reflection, followed by exploratory talk with a colleague, leading to the formulation of action plans. The process takes one hour.

Stage 1 **Personal work (15 minutes)**

Make a few notes about yourself with respect to your contribution to the work of the department and the institution in the past year, concentrating on the positive aspects. Using your own criteria will probably be most helpful to you. Or you can use some of the suggestions on *Handouts 1 and 2* overleaf.

Stage 2 **Pairs (15 minutes each)**

Talk through your thoughts and feelings with a partner of your choice, taking turns as speaker and listener.

(Listener: listen, ask for clarification, offer summaries etc. but don't prescribe, advise, make judgements etc.)

Stage 3 **Personal work (15 minutes)**

Work on *Handout 3: Action plans*. Make a contract with someone here if you think it will help. (For example, you can each agree to try out one of your plans by a certain date and to report back to the other.)

My contribution to the department/the Institution

1   as a teacher:

2   as a researcher:

3   as a thinker about my subject and about education:

4   as a problem-solver:

5

6

7

8

Handout 2

As far as your work in the institution/department/course is concerned, consider how you would like to develop in the areas listed below. Suggest for yourself a **specific** example for each area.

One way in which I would like to develop

a   in managing myself:

_____

b   in clarifying my personal value system and my personal goals:

_____

c   in being part of a more effective team:

_____

d   in continuing my own personal and professional development:

_____

e   in being more creative in my teaching:

_____

f   in being more effective at influencing people in my course team:

_____

g   in being a better manager:

_____

h   in improving as a supervisor to others:

_____

i

_____

Handout 3: Action plans

What I propose to do as a result of this activity.

1

2

3

When you have completed your list, choose one of your proposals and examine its implications by using the following diagram.

	for myself	involving others
payoffs		
sacrifices		

Observation checklist   **30**

Asking a colleague to come and sit in on your teaching seems a good way of appraising it. There are, however, certain precautions to be taken if the experience is to be a success. The inexperienced observer may have no notion of how to appraise your teaching and will tend to listen to the content and ignore the process. One expert listening to another can find it difficult to make useful comments about the learning experience of inexpert students.

For this reason, if you want evidence about your teaching from an observer, it is a good idea to use a checklist which focusses the observer's attention on specific aspects of the process. The simple observation sheet which follows is designed to be used by untrained observers. It encourages the observer to generate evidence, in the form of examples, rather than draw generalised conclusions directly from observation. Comments and judgements can come later after the evidence has been discussed.

Observation can be a one-sided business, with one person in a position of authority seeming to criticise the other. It can be made easier and more effective if it is undertaken on a reciprocal basis.

Observation sheet

Note down things you observe under each of the headings. Try to note enough detail to be able to describe specific incidents to the teacher afterwards.

Responsibility

Who took responsibility for the teaching? Who made the decisions about the content? Who made the decisions about the process? Who controlled the session?

Teaching strategies

What teaching strategies were used? Uninterrupted telling? Overviews? Repetition? Questioning? Testing? Setting problems? Debate? Checking on learning?

Learning strategies

What learning strategies did students use? Passive listening? Questioning? Note taking? Asking for more time? Who initiated the use of these learning strategies, the teacher or the students?

Feelings

What expressions or indications of feelings were there? Boredom? Excitement? Anxiety? Anger?

Problems

What problems were encountered? What were the critical incidents in the session and how were they handled?

An appraisal procedure 31

The procedure set out overleaf is designed for use in a situation where you have asked a colleague to sit in on one of your teaching sessions and give you some feedback. It may at first glance look unnecessarily complicated, but it follows a few simple and sensible principles.

It acknowledges the importance of preparation and the role of feelings. It starts with description before moving on to evaluation and action planning; this ensures that participants have the data in front of them before jumping to conclusions. It is organised so that the person being appraised has the opportunity to speak first at each stage; this encourages self discovery and protects self respect. It is also organised so that positive aspects are considered before negative; you can always find something positive to say, however badly a session went, and the worse it went the more important this is.

(This item was written with the help of David Jaques, Oxford Polytechnic.)

Appraisal procedure

	Teacher	Appraiser
Prior work	Provide the appraiser with any necessary papers etc.	Observe a teaching session and make notes
Feelings	Do you have any feelings about the teaching session (or about this feedback session) which you would like to express first?	Do you have any feelings about the teaching session (or about this feedback session) which you would like to express first?
Description	What did you notice about yourself and others during the session?	What did you notice about the teacher during the session?
Positive evaluation	What did you do well? How do you know? (Try to take content, process and outcomes separately.)	What did the teacher do well? How do you know? (Try to take content, process and outcomes separately.)
Negative evaluation	What didn't go so well? How do you know? (Try to take content, process and outcomes separately.)	What didn't go so well? How do you know? (Try to take content, process and outcomes separately.)
Action planning	In the light of the above, what do you propose to do differently another time?	What would you like the teacher to do differently another time?
Support	What can the appraiser, or others, do to help?	How may you be able to help?
Feedback to the appraiser	How helpful has the appraisal been?	
Feelings	Are there any feelings that still need to be expressed?	Are there any feelings that still need to be expressed?

Quality circles

32

Quality circles are small groups of workers in a company who meet regularly to discuss how to maintain or improve the quality of their product. The example most frequently cited is that of the Swedish car industry where the use of quality circles has brought about dramatic improvements. Groups of teachers can copy this model and set up quality circles which meet on an informal basis to appraise their teaching and plan improvements.

To set up a series of quality circle meetings, you first need to decide on a time and place. (In many institutions the lunch break is the best time; participants can bring their sandwiches and coffee.) Then you write to your colleagues to explain what quality circles are and to invite them to join you. In a large institution you may like to keep a mailing list of interested people.

You can give a focus to your meetings by choosing a specific topic each time, e.g. over-assessment, teaching large groups, improving students' use of the library, equal opportunities in the classroom etc. The discussion can be structured by the use of a short introductory paper or handout presented by one of the participants. (The paper here would not be meant to offer solutions or make proposals, but to raise an issue in order to get discussion going.) Or the format could be one of personal reflection:

The problem I used to face in my teaching was....

What I decided to do about it was....

What happened was....

What I will do next time is......

The advice I'd give to anyone wanting to copy these methods is....

Alternatively, you may want to hold no-agenda meetings, where the participants discuss whatever is important to them at the time. Such meetings can be started by each person in turn saying 'What's on top for me in my teaching at the moment is ....'

Whatever the format, it is helpful if the discussion is written up in some way. One of the participants could write a brief description of each meeting which is circulated to everyone on the mailing list, together with a reminder about the next meeting.

Sources of appraisal evidence

How do your students spend their time?

33

The way students choose to spend their study time is crucial to their success. The amount, nature and quality of their independent studying depends to a large extent on the way in which they are taught. So one way of appraising your teaching is to find out how your students spend their time.

The sorts of question which you may want to ask include:

    How much time do students spend studying?

    Which study tasks (or topics) are given priority?

    Which study tasks (or topics) are left out?

    What resources do students use (e.g. which books)?

    How long do specific tasks take (e.g. completing a problem sheet, reading a set chapter, writing a laboratory report)?

    How much reading do students do?

    How much preparation do students do for seminars?

It is important to ask such questions because it is clear that students allocate their time in very uneven ways and do not spend equal amounts of time on course components which carry equal weight in terms of assessment. Answers to the questions could help you to adjust your teaching by setting different tasks, suggesting different reading, stressing different topics, changing the balance of set work, and so on.

Members of a course team may also want information on how the students distribute their time between elements of the course. This will give an indication of ways in which the teachers vary in the demands they put on students. Some teachers, for example, specify precisely what students should do out of class while others provide little guidance. Some teaching, and especially some assessment schemes, seem to lead to routine busywork while others engage and stretch students intellectually. Elements of a course can also consume extra student time, simply by being more interesting.

Information on how students spend their time can be difficult to obtain. The reason for this is simple: students don't usually know. If you ask them about workloads in a questionnaire, they will usually either guess or work backwards from what seems to be expected of them. They need help if they are to make a realistic estimate.

The best way to find out how your students spend their time is to get them to keep a diary for a week, logging all their activities.

You will probably need to provide them with a pro forma and show them one which has been filled in (as in the example which follows) or they may record too little to be useful. You may need to label the pro forma with days of the week and remind students about their diaries every time you see them.

Anonymity is essential for this activity if students are not to falsify their entries. The use of an 'honest broker' **(see 26)** may be necessary to guarantee anonymity. Alternatively students in groups of four can pool the data from their diaries and hand in a summary of the 'averaged' activities of the four; they will benefit from the discussion and you will benefit from having the data summarised.

Knowledge of how they spend their time in itself helps students to change. You can help by adjusting your teaching and specifying what you expect them to do in their study time.

Study Diary

Course MLS II (term 2)

Day / Date Tues 13 Feb

Time	Study activity	Resources	Place
10·00–11·00	Went to lecture – took notes	Lecture handout	G 305
11·00–11·25	Chatted with friends – partly about using the microscope	Coffee	Students' Union
11·25–11·55	Went through lecture notes for first 4 lectures – tidied them up, read them, filled in a few gaps. Made a note to read ch. 3 of Smith + Smith	Lecture notes	S.U.
2·00 – 4·00	Practical	Apparatus etc.	Lab
4·20 – 5·00	Tried to read Smith & bloody Smith. Got bored. Gave up without finishing – and not even any useful notes.	Smith & Smith from Reserve Collection	Library

Total time on course   = 3 hrs

Total independent study time = 95 mins

Students' notes   34

When you are lecturing it can be hard to tell how much of what you are saying is getting across. In seminars and tutorials it can be difficult to guess what students are taking away with them. It is extremely hard to judge what students are getting out of their reading. But in all these situations students will be taking notes, and their notes can be very revealing.

Some courses require students to put all their notes together into a portfolio and to submit this for assessment. Such portfolios can give a clear indication of the quality of students' engagement with the course, and show which parts of it grab their attention and which cause problems.

A less comprehensive approach, but one which is also valuable, is to ask individual students to let you see their note books and files from time to time. If you give them warning ('Next week I'm going to collect in your notes') they may well 'fake good', which won't tell you much. So you should make these requests randomly. Students will co-operate if you tell them at the start of your course that such random requests will be made.

Students' marks

Ostensibly, the purpose of marks is to indicate student performance. Marks can also, of course, be used to appraise the performance of teachers.

Heads of department often use results as a criterion for appraising the teacher, particularly where courses are examined by external bodies. And students will select the option where it's supposed to be easiest to get high marks. Instead of leaving the appraisal of your teaching to their impressionistic judgements, you may prefer to carry out an analysis of the marks yourself.

Before you undertake your analysis, you may need to get advice from a colleague who understands statistics. You will want to know whether you have enough data to be able to draw valid conclusions and whether the questions you want to ask are appropriate for the data you have. If your marks are already on the computer, this of course makes the whole process much quicker and easier.

You can use this analysis to make comparisons, for example, between elements of a course, between types of assessment, between markers, between students (male/ female, black/white, mature/school leaver etc.) or between this year's results and previous years'.

Any discrepancy which cannot be explained by real differences in student performance may indicate something about your teaching or it may say something about your marking. Either way it is unjust to students and needs to be followed up, individually or departmentally.

Teaching methods audit 36

Academic courses are generally designed to be balanced in terms of their content, but are often unbalanced in terms of their process. On one polytechnic degree course, for example, students' class contact time varies from 24% to 55% of their total study time, depending on which combinations of subjects they choose. Some students are timetabled for four times as many lectures as others and six times as many seminars. These differences tend to occur accidentally rather than as the result of the careful selection of teaching methods to suit educational goals; methods are generally chosen by the individual teachers responsible for particular course elements and nobody has a clear overall picture of the situation.

If you want to get an overview of the teaching methods on your course you can carry out an audit where you collect and collate evidence of how much teaching is going on and what form it takes. The course team can then start working towards a balance of methods.

The basic information for the audit may be available in course documentation, such as CNAA or B/TEC submissions, e.g.

Lectures	20 hours
Seminars	10 hours
Practicals	18 hours
Tutorials	2 hours
Total teaching	50 hours

If the information is not readily available, you will need to ask your colleagues to supply it. You can help them by giving them a pro forma to fill in, e.g.

Teaching method used	Hours per year
Workshops	....
Lectures	....
Seminars	....
Tutorials	....
Practicals	....
Other (please specify)	....
Total class contact	....

signed...

It can also be instructive to look at the results of a teaching methods audit in combination with evidence of how students spend their study time **(see 33)**.

Assessment audit 37

Assessment, more than any other factor, determines how and what students study. No appraisal of a course would be complete without an appraisal of its assessment system.

Look out for possible anomalies, distortions and injustices in your assessment system. You can test them out by doing an audit and comparing assessment methods and results. This will only work, however, if you are clear about the questions you want to ask.

A list of ideas for assessment audits, together with suggested questions, follows.

a   **Coursework**

List the number and types of coursework assignments set for each element of the course.

Is the workload in any element significantly heavier or lighter?

b   **Assessment methods**

Review the assessment methods used.

Is there a logical progression in the sophistication and novelty of assessments which matches students' development?

c   **Weighting**

List the weightings of equivalent pieces of coursework in different elements of the course.

Are any unnecessarily higher or lower than others?

d   **Educational objectives**

Identify the educational objectives which are being assessed in eac assignment.

Do the objectives follow a logical progression which matches the development c the course?

See also **Students' marks (35).**

Letters 38

One way of finding out what students think of your course is to ask them to write you a letter. This method of appraisal is comparable with the student questionnaire, and in particular with the instant questionnaire **(see 6)**, but it encourages students to respond in a more direct and informal manner. They are familiar with the letter as a means of communication and find it easy to write one.

This activity need take only five minutes at the end of a lecture or seminar. You could say, 'I'd like to know what you think of the course so far, so I suggest that you all write me a letter about it. Just take a piece of paper and write "Dear Graham ..." and then say whatever it is you want to say to me about the course'.

Though you will not be able to draw any statistical conclusions from the letters you receive, this method of appraisal does mean that your students give you the feedback which they want to give you, about the issues which they have selected themselves and in the language which they have chosen to use.

Teaching logs

A teaching log is a detailed record of how you spend your time as a teacher. It entails noting down how much of your working day you spend on each of your teaching activities: lecturing, preparing classes, marking, reading etc.

Using a log is one of the simplest ways of reflecting on what you actually do as a teacher. It gives you insights into your daily behaviour which can help you to improve your teaching. It will also provide you with evidence which can be used in an appraisal interview.

The type of log is a matter of personal choice: you can write shorthand key words, brief comments or full descriptions. It is important, however, that you write up your log regularly, as accurately as you can, and over as long a period as you can. You also have a choice of format: your log can consist of jottings in a note book or it can be written according to a pro forma. An illustration of one pro forma follows.

The analysis of your log can be undertaken in a variety of ways. Some examples follow.

a Go through several weeks' entries looking for patterns in the way you teach, and events and thoughts which recur.

b Note the strengths and weaknesses in your teaching which your log reveals.

c Ask a colleague to read your log, or persuade a colleague to keep a similar log and read each other's. Give each other feedback.

A teaching log can be especially useful when undertaking action research **(see 45)**.

Teaching log

Day...   Date ....

Details of teaching sessions, preparation, marking, meetings etc.	Comments and reflections
Early morning	
8.00	
9.00	
10.00	
11.00	
12.00	
1.00	
2.00	
3.00	
4.00	
5.00	
6.00	
Early evening	
Night-time	

Teaching profiles   **40**

A teaching profile is a collection of material which provides an overview or profile of an individual's teaching. Creating a teaching profile involves collecting evidence over a period of time, and organising it under various headings. A teaching profile cannot be created overnight: it means getting into the habit of being systematic about keeping teaching records.

A profile can be used as a source of evidence for appraising teaching and would provide an ideal basis, together with archive material **(see 41 Archiving)**, for preparation for an annual appraisal interview. The following list of categories, taken from the TES guide to submitting teaching profiles[1], illustrates a range of possible sources of evidence.

Suggested contents of a teaching profile

Concerning aims and objectives

1   Course aims and objectives

Concerning teaching methods

2   Range and level of teaching

3   Pattern of teaching methods used

4   Special teaching methods used

5   Course materials prepared for students

6   Use of special learning resources

7   Availability to students

8   Identification of special difficulties

---

1   G Gibbs,   *Creating a Teaching Profile*,
                      TES, Bristol, 1988

Concerning assessment and evaluation

Assessment methods

9   Range of assessment methods

10   Provision of feedback to students

11   Reliability of assessment

Evidence of outcomes of teaching

12   Student grades

13   Products of student learning

14   Student publications, awards or exhibitions

15   Student progress to more advanced courses

16   External examiners' reports

Evaluation evidence

17   Course evaluation procedures

18   Course evaluation data

19   Evidence from student, department or institutionally organised evaluation

20   Unsolicited written evidence

21   Action research

Concerning the continued study of teaching and learning

22   Record of innovations in teaching

23   Reading of journals and other literature on teaching

24   Teaching qualifications, courses and conferences attended

25   Review of new teaching materials

26   Use of teaching support services

27   Participation in in-house seminars on teaching

28   Participation in course development

29   Pursuit of a line of research which contributes directly to teaching

30   The presentation of a textbook or other instructional material

31   Publication of articles concerned with teaching

32   Contribution to the teaching of one's subject at a national level

33   Involvement in teaching development within the institution

---

A teaching profile created for a specific purpose, such as an annual interview, would obviously not contain items from every section: it would need to be selective and the items would need to be short. Any extensive material would be best contained in an appendix. For example:

8   Identification of special difficulties

'On course 997 (Introduction to Egyptology) many students experienced great difficulty with the somewhat daunting reading material. Evaluation (see Appendix 2) showed students to be reading little and gaining little from what they read. In 1986 I introduced a series of reading guides (see Appendix 3 for an example) and since 1987 I have held two reading workshops at the start of each term. These workshops are now attended by students on other courses in the department. Evaluation (see Appendix 4) has shown that the quantity, at least, of student reading has increased markedly.

(The material in the appendices in this example would already be on file, ready to be used for this purpose.)

Strategies for collecting evidence

4 1   Archiving

4 2   Triangulation

4 3   Progressive focussing

4 4   Goal-free appraisal

4 5   Action research

4 6   Serendipity

Archiving

Teachers like to know that they are developing their skills over time. This progress, however, can be difficult to quantify: it is hard to remember exactly the quality of a lecture or seminar which happened a year or more ago.

One solution to this problem is to develop techniques for 'archiving' performance, or the appraisal of performance, for future reference. This can be done using a range of media: written data, computer-based systems or video recordings.

a   **Using written data**

Appraisal documentation can include summaries of questionnaire returns, notes on self and peer appraisal, analyses of students' marks and details of decisions taken at staff development interviews. Material needs to be recorded system- atically, updated regularly and filed according to year and course so that comparisons can easily be made.

b   **Using computer-based systems**

Micro-computers and word-processing have brought the easy storage and retrieval of appraisal data within the reach of all teachers and there are numerous evaluation questionnaires which can be run on simple machines. (See the section on questionnaires, and especially items 1, 2 and 5.)

c   **Using video recordings**

Now that simple video recording systems are commonplace in educational instit- utions, teachers can easily film 'live' performances in lectures, seminars and tutorials. These recordings can form part of an archive of evidence of the development of classroom skills and be used for immediate and long-term self appraisal. They can also be presented at appraisal interviews.

Triangulation 42

Triangulation is a research strategy in which results are obtained from a range of different perspectives. When appraising your teaching, you will get a fuller and more accurate picture if you bring together evidence from several sources, such as colleagues, present students and past students, or if you use a variety of methods, such as questionnaires **(see Section 1)**, interviews **(see 15)** and diaries **(see 33 and 39)**.

Progressive focussing   43

It is not possible to appraise all the teaching and learning on your courses all at once: the task would be too complex and too time-consuming. You may also not be clear at the outset which aspects are worth investigating. Then there is the problem of choosing whether to go for breadth, and risk not getting enough detail, or for depth, and risk missing important issues.

Progressive focussing is a useful investigative strategy which begins with a wide scope and progressively narrows down the focus of the investigation. Each stage brings with it a more detailed picture. Once an issue has been explored in sufficient depth to inform changes, the focus can be broadened again and a new issue tackled.

In the appraisal of teaching, you may find that it takes several stages of progressive focussing even to discover what the problems are. You will probably also find that different evaluation methods will be appropriate at the different stages.

To illustrate progressive focussing in practice, a description of its use in a polytechnic science department follows. (The aim was to evaluate a three-year degree programme.)

Stage 1   A small group of third year students was interviewed about the course in order to find out what they thought were the most important issues. The interview was conducted by an 'honest broker' **(see 26)** in an open and unstructured way. About thirty issues were thrown up.

Stage 2   A small group of lecturers from the department selected about twenty of these issues to follow up. A 'hypothesis testing' questionnaire **(see 12)** was used with all third year students, to find out which of the issues they felt strongly about. This revealed one issue of overriding importance: students felt that the optional course components made unequal demands on them.

Stage 3   The coursework demands of all options were examined by the group of lecturers. It was found that students were being asked to undertake more demanding tasks in some options than in others and that the proportion of coursework marks allocated to set tasks was largely unrelated to their size. Some rationalisation of coursework demands took place.

Stage 4   All three years of the degree course were surveyed in order to discover how students perceived the relative demands of options **(see 9)**. Students were asked to rate every option for its workload, intellectual demand, and so on. About a dozen options with atypical ratings were highlighted for more detailed study.

Stage 5   At this point department-wide evaluation could go no further and individual lecturers had to take responsibility for self-appraisal and the detailed implementation of changes. Those lecturers responsible for the atypical options were asked to find out what was giving rise to these ratings. Evaluations were undertaken in a variety of ways, some by the lecturers themselves, some through reciprocal arrangements **(see Section 4)** and some by an 'honest broker' **(see 26)**. The evaluations identified specific causes of variation in demands and led to context-specific changes (e.g. reducing the number of laboratory reports required in one of the options, moving some course content from one option to another etc). The effects of these changes were evaluated the following year.

(See also 2 Diagnostic questionnaire.)

Goal-free appraisal   44

Systematic appraisal involves checking whether the aims and objectives of a course have been met. And appraisal generally is directed towards exploring areas which have been defined beforehand, often by people who are too close to the course to see what the important issues are.

Goal-free appraisal, on the other hand, attempts simply to find out what is going on. The appraiser tries to be completely open-minded about what to look at and report on. For this reason goal-free appraisal really requires a neutral outsider to be the appraiser **(see 26 Honest Broker)**.

Such an outsider might notice, for example, that social relationships on the course seem to be poor, that practical work appears to be treated in a mechanical and unreflective way, and that teachers are perceived by students to care more about their own research and consultancy than about undergraduate teaching. None of these points may be directly related to course objectives, but all of them are important.

It can be difficult for teachers to accept the findings of an external appraiser, so the two parties need to get together beforehand to talk about the purposes and possible outcomes of the exercise.

Action research   45

Action research is experimentation undertaken by teachers as a part of their everyday teaching. It can be as rigorous as conventional research and contribute to formal theory building. Or, as here, it can be informal appraisal carried out by teachers in order to improve their understanding of their own teaching and develop their teaching techniques.

Action research involves a simple cyclical process of observing what happens in your teaching and reflecting on these observations, finding explanations for what happened, and planning improvements. Trying out your plan then gives you a new experience and a new source of observation and reflection. It is a similar process to scientific method, but the data is your own experience, and the theories which emerge, though they may be based on educational psychology, are personal theories.

The flow chart overleaf illustrates the cycle and also provides instructions for each stage of the process.

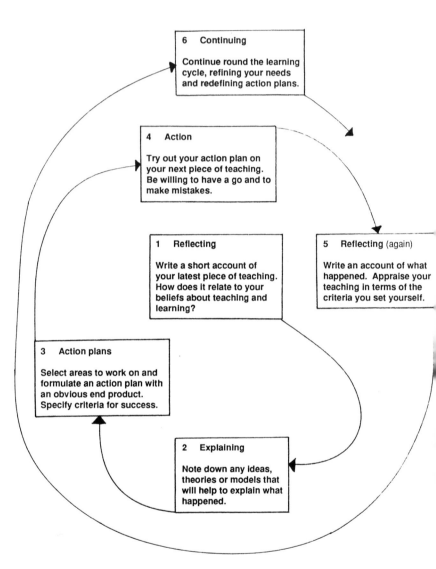

6   Continuing

Continue round the learning cycle, refining your needs and redefining action plans.

4   Action

Try out your action plan on your next piece of teaching. Be willing to have a go and to make mistakes.

1   Reflecting

Write a short account of your latest piece of teaching. How does it relate to your beliefs about teaching and learning?

5   Reflecting (again)

Write an account of what happened. Appraise your teaching in terms of the criteria you set yourself.

3   Action plans

Select areas to work on and formulate an action plan with an obvious end product. Specify criteria for success.

2   Explaining

Note down any ideas, theories or models that will help to explain what happened.

The Action Research Planner

Serendipity 46

In addition to the feedback which is formally requested through questionnaires and other means, there is any amount of unsolicited appraisal which is available to those who are alert to it. This type of appraisal includes such data as students' body language in class, informal letters from past students or employers and reported gossip (e.g. 'Students say they're enjoying your lectures'). If students put on a revue or produce a newspaper or alternative handbook, this too will be full of information about their perceptions of how they are taught. There is also unsolicited feedback which is more quantifiable: the number of your colleagues who request or decline to work with you, for example, or the proportion of students who sign on for your options or who ask you to supervise their projects.

Serendipity is normally frowned on as a way of appraising your teaching because it is haphazard, incomplete and unreliable but it needs to be taken seriously because it is the most common method of appraisal used by teachers and heads of department alike.

Look out for unsolicited feedback and notice how much you rely on it. Check out rumours and hearsay by following them up with questionnaires and other formal methods of appraisal. And ask your head of department to give you the source of any evidence which is used (either for or against you) in an appraisal interview.

Appraisal interviews

Annual reviews   47

It is common for formal appraisal schemes to include some kind of annual stock-taking. Teachers are expected to undertake a review of the past year and to bring this appraisal evidence to an interview with a superior, such as the head of department, or to a group meeting with colleagues.

The list below shows the headings of an annual review form from a polytechnic department. The form is used to help lecturers to summarise their main activities and achievements in preparation for the staff development interview with their head of department. At first glance this may look like a typical form covering a comprehensive range of activities. While it may be typical, however, it is not comprehensive: it does not contain a single item concerned with teaching, even though teaching is the main activity of most lecturers.

Annual Review Form

1   In-house job development
    1.1   Course development
    1.2   Personal skills development
    1.3   New administrative responsibilities
2   Publications
3   Research
4   Papers presented at conferences
5   Short courses and conferences attended
6   Consultancy and professional practice
7   Local community activities
8   Membership of committees
9   Work for degrees and other qualifications
10   Other activities (e.g. development of overseas links)
11   Polytechnic/departmental resources received in support of staff development activities

---

The checklist below, by comparison, focusses on teaching. The earlier sections of this book have described a wide variety of methods for undertaking the informal appraisal of your teaching. This checklist is designed to help you to summarise your achievements and organise your evidence, though you may wish to use it selectively and concentrate on those aspects you would most like to discuss in the interview.

Appraisal of teaching for year ....

---

1   **Steps taken to improve teaching methods/skills,** e.g. attendance at seminars, short courses or conferences concerned with teaching, observation of your own or others' teaching, support from educational development unit, development projects undertaken etc.

2   **Teaching, learning and assessment methods introduced,** including changes made in response to previous appraisal.

3   **Course and teaching evaluation evidence collected,** e.g. summaries and data from questionnaire surveys undertaken, with comparative data from other courses or previous years if possible.

4   **Scholarship concerned with teaching,** e.g. regular reading of journals concerned with the teaching of your subject, presentation of conference paper on teaching, research project based on your teaching, publication of article on teaching etc.

5   **Planned changes in your teaching,** including steps to achieve these changes, e.g. application for financial support, visits to other institutions or conferences.

Preparing your appraiser

48

It often happens that both the appraiser and the teacher come away from an appraisal meeting feeling dissatisfied. There are many different kinds of reason for this but probably the most common cause is that neither party makes appropriate preparations for the meeting, so that appraisal evidence is lacking, opportunities are missed and mistakes are made.

You can help your appraisal interview to be a success by not only preparing for it yourself but also by letting your appraiser know in advance, preferably in writing, what expectations you have for the interview and how you would like him/her to prepare for it. Some suggestions follow.

Get the timing right
'Please arrange the interview late enough in the year to allow me to collect evidence about my teaching, but early enough to allow me to introduce changes for the following year.'
'Please arrange the interview a full year ahead of my application to go through the efficiency bar.'

Get advance warning
'Please give me at least two weeks' notice so that we can both prepare.'

Get a definition of evidence
'What kinds of evidence about the quality of teaching do you find convincing?'
'What evidence will you bring to the meeting?'

Clarify the purpose of the interview and the procedure
'I'd like a brief chat beforehand so we can both be clear what the interview will be for

and how it will be handled.'

Provide documentation (e.g. *Appraisal of teaching* form described in item 47)
'I've enclosed a brief review of my teaching over the past year which I'd like you to read through before the meeting. If this documentation isn't appropriate, please let me know straight away.'

Avoid being put at a disadvantage (e.g. sitting in a low chair looking up at your appraiser over a huge desk)
'I'd appreciate it if we could meet in my office.'

Avoid interruptions
'I've cleared my diary and arranged to divert telephone calls. I've got a *Do Not Disturb* notice for my door so we shouldn't be interrupted.'

Suggest an agenda
'I suggest the following agenda:
1   I review my teaching year and provide you with evidence for my self-appraisal.
2   You comment and add your perceptions, backing them up with your evidence.
3   I outline my plans for next year and describe what support I'd like.
4   You explain your plans for the Department for the year and how you see me within those plans. (Of course if you let me see these plans beforehand it would save us both a lot of time.)
5   We negotiate about what I will concentrate on in the coming year and how you will support me.
6   We write down an agreed outcome, including:
    -    my teaching duties
    -    my development needs
    -    your support'

Suggest ground rules

'I suggest that we:

- share the interview time equally

- concentrate on my strengths and my development

- back up all our observations with evidence'

Suggest confidentiality

'I suggest that everything that takes place in the interview is confidential and that all notes we take are confidential.'

You may also find it helpful to show your appraiser this book, explain how you have used it and suggest that you both follow some of the suggestions.

The appraisal interview in context

49

Your decisions about how you will appraise your teaching and present your self-appraisal need to be made in the context of departmental and institutional plans and any assumptions which have been made about the way you fit into these plans. For example, there may not be much point in presenting a detailed appraisal of your teaching on a course which your head of department secretly intends to axe. Nor may it be very productive to prepare a case for study leave if you have been quietly pencilled in to lead a new degree programme.

You may be lucky and work in an environment where such plans are openly negotiated in a democratic way, by all those affected. If you are not so lucky you will need to get hold of information well before your interview. A checklist of questions follows.

a   Is there a departmental development plan or any written statement about the department's future?

b   Is there a staff development plan with clear goals? Is there an organised programme of sabbaticals, secondments and training, or is it a free-for-all? Are there clear criteria for selection?

c   Which administrative jobs will need filling next year? (Admissions? Examinations?)

d   What possibilities exist for promotion? What are the criteria for promotion?

e   What committees or working parties is it useful to belong to? (Academic Board? Research Committee?)

f   What funding or relief from duties is available from within the institution? What sorts of developments are funded?

g   What would your head of department **like** you to be doing next year?

There are also questions about appraisal itself which need to be checked out.

h Who has a stake in your appraisal? Is it only the department or does the faculty have a stake, or the institution? How about your professional body, the CNAA, your colleagues and your home life? Find out how narrowly the canvas is being drawn and challenge this narrowness.

i What is your institution's formal and legal position on appraisal (for example regarding your contract of employment)? How does this relate to employment legislation? Can your union inform you of your rights?

j How does your appraisal relate to your promotion prospects? Are written records kept which will be used in promotion decisions?

Attitudes and expectations

50

It isn't much fun being an appraiser. Teachers often approach the appraisal interview in a negative way: they come unprepared, show little willingness to change and display a wholly defensive attitude. As a result the appraisers too become defensive and expect appraisal interviews to be difficult.

Anything you can offer your appraiser in terms of a positive attitude will probably be welcomed and will make the interview easier for both of you. Some suggestions follow.

a   **Demonstrate that you are taking appraisal seriously.**
    Give the interview your serious attention.

b   **Demonstrate that you have prepared for the interview.**
    Send your appraiser documentation about your teaching in advance so that it can be read before the interview. Give your appraiser notice of any plans or suggestions you have.

c   **Demonstrate that you do not intend to spring an ambush.**
    Give your appraiser notice of requests for resources, time off or relief from duties.

d   **Demonstrate a willingness to identify and tackle problems.**
    Be open about problems which have been unearthed. Suggest ways forward and ask for support.

e   **Demonstrate a willingness to give and take.**
    Be prepared to negotiate. If you offer to solve a problem for your appraiser (like agreeing to review problematic assessment procedures) your appraiser may be

more willing to solve some of your problems (like reducing some of your administrative duties).

f   **Demonstrate that you are prepared to be reasonable.**

Be realistic about what your appraiser can and cannot do to help you. (It may not be possible for the cramped laboratory to be rebuilt this year.) Your appraiser may then be more willing to be realistic about making demands on you.

Records of appraisal interviews 51

It is important to have a record of appraisal interviews so that both you and your appraiser know and remember what has been agreed. Without a record, there may be mistrust on both sides and next year you will be starting from scratch again.

You may fear that your interview will be inconclusive, that recorded comments may be biased or unsubstantiated, and stored in files you do not have access to, or used for purposes you do not approve of. If so you may find it helpful to make some of the following suggestions to your appraiser.

The record of an appraisal interview should be written at the meeting. It should include basic factual information (names, place, time, status of meeting etc). It should reflect the views of both of you and refer to evidence which backs up these views. The statement should conclude with a clear agreement on action to be taken by both of you. (Where agreement proves impossible, a named person can be asked to arbitrate.) Both you and your appraiser should read, agree and sign this statement at the meeting and keep a copy to use as the basis of next year's appraisal. The appraiser should make no record of the meeting apart from the agreed statement, which should be confidential and used for no purpose other than appraisal.

Practising for the interview 52

An appraisal interview can be tense and difficult, sometimes just because it is unfamiliar. Experience with job or promotion interviews doesn't necessarily help. You can improve your appraisal interview performance and reduce anxieties by practising for the interview beforehand.

The best way to do this is to agree with a colleague to interview each other. The following suggestions are designed to help you get the maximum benefit from this dry run.

a   Prepare yourself and your documentation as for the real interview **(see items 47, 48 and 49)**.

b   Have your colleague play the role of your head of department, or whoever will be your appraiser. Then swop roles and interview your colleague. Try to stay 'in role' throughout your practice interview; you can leave discussion until afterwards.

c   Allow plenty of time for discussion at the end of the interview. Review your performance and ask your colleague for feedback. You may like to use the following questions.

What did you achieve in the interview?

What problems did you have? (e.g. Were there any questions you couldn't answer? Were you short of any documentation?)

Who controlled the interview?

What was the outcome of the interview? Was it the outcome you wanted?

How can you usefully prepare for the real interview?

Personal development contracts   53

Ideally your appraisal interview will lead to a clear agreement on action to be taken by both you and your appraiser **(see 51 Records of appraisal interviews)**. Whether or not this happens you may also wish to have a more detailed statement of what you intend to achieve over the coming year: a personal development contract. Such a contract typically runs to two pages of notes and is probably best arranged under headings:

Teaching

Research

Consultancy

Scholarship/writing

   publications

   reading

   learning

Personal

   physical

   social

   home

You can devise your own personal development contract, where you specify what you aim to achieve over the coming year. Or, better still, you can arrange to agree contracts with a colleague or in a group.

One of the authors of this book meets once a year with a group of colleagues who review personal development contracts produced a year before, and draw up contracts for the following year. Members of the group evaluate their achievements and criticise each other's contracts, suggesting where plans may be over-ambitious, where tightening up on the wording may make goals clearer etc. Finally they sign each other's contracts as a way of indicating a group commitment to taking contracts seriously.